ACKNOWLEDGMENTS

This magazine has been published by Wharncliffe Magazines in association with Pen and Sword Military Books Limited, with the purpose of creating an awarness and an interest in the Somme battles of 1916.

For nearly twenty years Pen and Sword has published numerous books covering various Pals battalions, formed for the 'Big Push'. They have also been fore-runners in setting up the Battleground Series guides, which are packed with then and now illustrations, using battle maps from the time and road maps of the sites today. They are all specifically designed to take the tourer safely through these now historic sites. Many more books have been written and published by Pen and Sword on the battles of the First World War.

All of these publications would not have been possible if it had not been for the skill and dedication of our authors who have painstakingly researched and then written about these subjects in order to bring these historic events to light. Extracts have been taken from a number of these titles to produce this magazine.

Only a small portion relating to the 1st July 1916 has been taken from each book appearing in this publication. Much more information can been gleaned from reading about the events of the Somme battles and the awful aftermath of the day through reading the books mentioned at the end of each extract.

Pen and Sword Military Books would like to thank; Peter Hart, Nigel Cave, Jack Horsfall, Roni Wilkinson, Michael Stedman, Valmai and Tonie Holt, Jack Sheldon and Richard van Emden, whose works have appeared in this magazine SOMME THE BATTLE NINETY YEARS ON.

Wharncliffe
HISTORY MAGAZINES

In association with;

Pen & Sword Military Books.

First published in Great Britain in 2006 by
Wharncliffe History Magazines
47 Church Street
Barnsley
South Yorkshire
S70 2AS

Copyright © Wharncliffe Publishing, 2006

Design, layout & photograph colouring:
Jon Wilkinson

ISBN: 1 84415 472 6

Printed and bound in the United Kingdom

For a complete list of Pen & Sword titles please
contact
PEN & SWORD BOOKS LIMITED
47 Church Street, Barnsley, South Yorkshire,
S70 2AS, England
E-mail: enquiries@pen-and-sword.co.uk
Website: www.pen-and-sword.co.uk

CONTENTS

INTRODUCTION By Jon Wilkinson

The year 1914 was to change mankind in every way. It was a beginning that gave birth to great advancements in technology that altered the way man fought his wars. For the first time in human civilization he had learned to kill in the skies, under the sea, under the battlefield as well as on it. He learned how to bring death to millions on a scale never known, by the use of machine guns, artillery, poisoned gas and for the first time, aircraft. But for people of the British Empire, 1914 was not the only year that was to become a turning point in their lives.

1st July 1916 saw a campaign that devastated the lives of thousands of many young men, many under age, serving under the British Empire. It was a day chosen to begin what had been called the 'Big Push', a desperate attempt to overwhelm the German Front Line and bring an end to a two year long stalemate on the Western Front.

It has become hard to believe that we have reached the ninetieth anniversary of the Somme battle. For many, accounts of that day would have been passed on to them by their fathers or grandfathers but as the years have moved on the veterans have faded and now their stories can only be told in written accounts. The Battle of the Somme has become tightly woven into the memory of the British nation and stands as a testimony to the conflict which took the lives of thousands of working class men. Towns, cities and even villages, bear some sort of memorial of remembrance to a sacrificed youth drawn from its own communities.

A soldier on the battlefield, shrouded in fog and confusion, can only relate what happened in one corner of a very large picture, it may be a disjointed account of events, but it then takes a military historian to study the events and piece together using various sources from all sides to clarify the facts.

This publication, SOMME: THE BATTLEFIELD NINETY YEARS ON, has been designed to ressurect an interest in the events leading up to the Somme battle and re-introduce old and current books covering this topic in depth. Various well known military authors have painstakingly researched the events and studied not only the politics of the day but also the young men who answered the call to join Kitchener's Army. Some have supplied detailed accounts taken from reports and have then constructed a tour which will take the reader onto the battlefields and help them retrace the movement of battle. Their books have been supported by photographs of the fields taken then and now and then backed up with maps and diagrams to take the reader step by step over the killing grounds, much of which have become tranquil farm land and meadows.

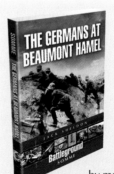

MAJOR & MRS HOLT'S BATTLEFIELD GUIDES

'Invaluable in the field' – *The Daily Telegraph*

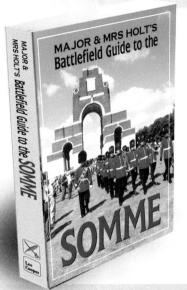

HOLT'S BATTLEFIELD GUIDE TO THE SOMME

Major and Mrs Holt's Battlefield Guide to the Somme is one of the bestselling guide books to the battlefields of the Somme. The guide includes four recommended, timed itineraries representing one day's travelling. Every stop on route has an accompanying description and often a tale of heroic or tragic action. Memorials, private and official, sites of memorable conflict, the resting places of personalities of note are all drawn together with sympathetic and understanding commentary that gives the reader a sensitivity towards the events of 1916.

INCLUDES A LARGE, FULL COLOUR MAP

ISBN: **0 85052 414 8** • Price: **£14.95**

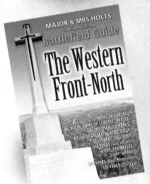

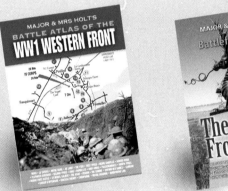

HOLT'S CONCISE ILLUSTRATED BATTLEFIELD GUIDES TO: THE WESTERN FRONT - NORTH

Together with the guide to the Western Front - South, the Western Front - North form s the most comprehensive and detailed English-language guides to the WW1 Western Front ever produced. The books follow the same tried and tested formula as the rest of the series of a timed and measured itinerary with historic and anecdotal information at each stop.

ISBN: **0 85052 933 6** • Price: **£14.99**

HOLT'S POCKET GUIDE TO THE SOMME

This book is designed conveniently in a small size, for those who have only limited time to visit, or who are simply interested in as an introduction to the historic battlefields. The book contains many full colour maps and photographs and detailed instructions on what to see and where to visit.

ISBN: **1 84415 400 9** • Price: **£6.99**

HOLT'S BATTLE ATLAS TO WW1

Having spent 35 years travelling around the battlefield of the Western Front, the Holts' have produced many battlemaps for tourists and battlefield travellers. This book now represents a culmination of all that work. Each map is tried and tested and accompanied by a short description of the battle.

ISBN: **1 84415 400 9** • Price: **£9.99** *published August*

THE WESTERN FRONT - SOUTH

This guide contains many fascinating but little-visited areas by travellers. Many of them have lain virtually 'dormant' for many years but have recently been renovated and opened up by dedicated local enthusiasts. Each battlefield starts with some pertinent quotations by participants, has a succinct Summary of the Battle, Opening Moves and What Happened sections and then a Battlefield Tour.

ISBN: **1 84415 239 1** • Price: **£15.99**

ORDER NOW!
TEL: 01226 734555

ONLINE: **www.pen-and-sword.co.uk**

PEN & SWORD BOOKS • 47 CHURCH STREET • BARNSLEY • S70 2AS

THE
SOMME
BATTLEFIELD
1916

An official history map showing the Somme battlefield and the ever shifting lines of engagement from 1st July to 17th November 1916.

REFERENCE.

Enemy original system of defence	—
Our original front of attack	—
Line reached and maintained 1st July	—
Line reached in fighting between 2nd & 13th July	—
Our second advance—14th July	—
Line held—12th September	—
" " 18th "	—
" " 27th "	—
" " 17th November	—

THE SOMME BATTLEFIELD 2006

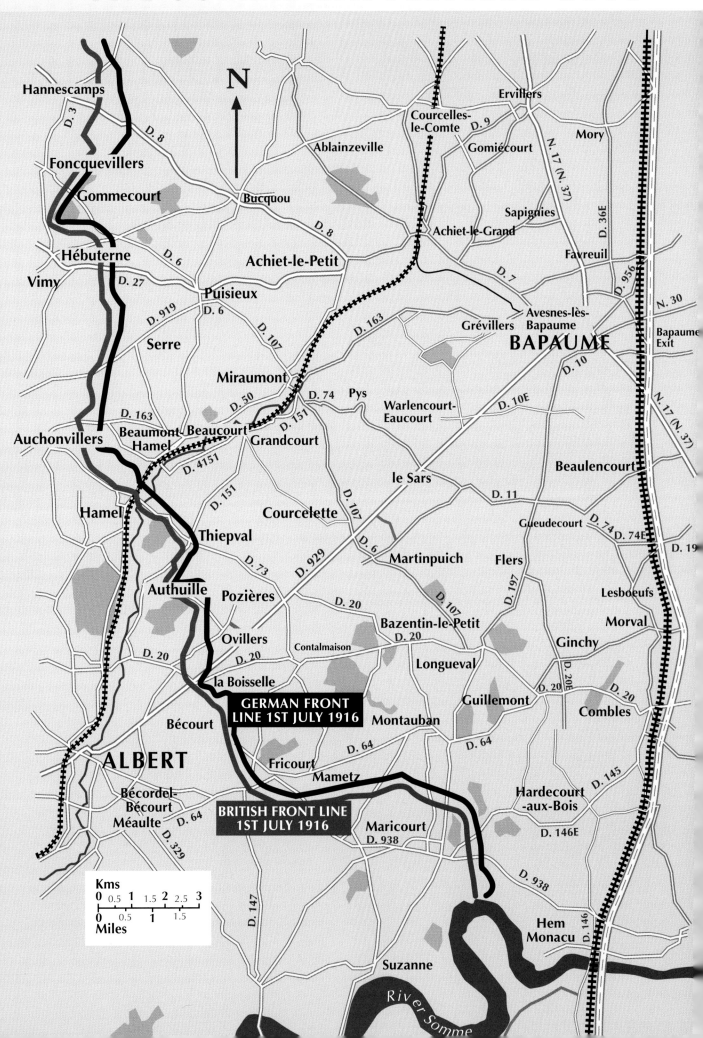

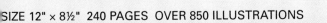

'You watched the battery and you saw the flash of the guns. You then knew pretty well exactly how many seconds it would take for those shells to arrive at the target. You then shifted the wing of your aeroplane to have an unrestricted view of the target and you saw the fall of the shell or shells.'

CAPTAIN ARCHIBALD JAMES
2 SQUADRON, RFC

12

SOMME SUCCESS – THE NEW BATTLEFIELD IN THE AIR–1916

Over thousands of years conflict had been waged on land and sea, but in the First World War a new battleground was found as war took to the air. Flying was still a new phenomenon: Orville and Wilbur Wright had first flown an aircraft in December 1903, the Royal Flying Corps (RFC) was only founded in 1912 and just sixty-three assorted aircraft in four squadrons had accompanied the British Expeditionary Force into action in August 1914. In retrospect it is amazing how quickly the RFC matured under the overwhelming imperatives forced on it by the Great War.

By Peter Hart

This article was extracted from *Somme Success* and is reproduced here by permission of Pen and Sword Books Ltd.

The original function of the RFC had been one of visual reconnaissance, in essence as an adjunct to the cavalry. A pilot, an observer and his trusty notebook had been the norm. Simple messages recording German movements were either dropped in message bags or personally handed to the Headquarters staff. But as the continuous trench lines developed, reconnaissance missions took on an ever-greater importance. Aircraft were left as the only method of finding out what was going on behind the German front line. In an effort to maximize the information brought back from each reconnaissance mission experimental cameras were taken up in the aircraft.

Although early photographs were usually blurred, where military requirements led, technology soon followed slavishly. The humble notebook was abandoned in favour of the increasingly pin-sharp glass plate photographs which recorded details that would have eluded even the most sharp-eyed of observers in flight. The bulky cameras were clamped to the outside of the cockpit and resulted in a photographic 'map' of everything directly below the aircraft. In addition, prior to any ground offensive, 'oblique' photographs taken with the camera held at an angle of roughly 15 to 45 degrees, were also highly prized by the infantry officers for the detail they could give of the hidden ground across which they would soon be advancing. The art of photographic interpretation was born: German gun batteries were found to be visible even when camouflaged, machine-gun posts stood revealed, dugout entrances, footpaths, headquarters and changes in trench systems – all were immediately obvious to the experts.

EYES IN THE SKY

But photographs were not the sum total of the RFC contribution. Once the technological problems of getting a wireless transmitter and aerial aloft in an aircraft had been overcome, it was only natural to use them for artillery observation. Fertile minds soon solved the conundrum of one-way communication and, with the introduction of the ubiquitous clock-code, an aircraft could provide the corrections that would range shells directly onto targets that were completely invisible from the guns or their forward observation posts on the ground.

You watched the battery and you saw the flash of the guns. You then knew pretty well exactly how many

A British BE2 C biplane fitted with a camera for aerial photography.

whether they were falling at one o'clock or three o'clock from the target; and the distance as expressed in the imaginary circles which you visualised without much difficulty. With a good battery – batteries varied enormously – you should get them right on target at about the third salvo.

CAPTAIN ARCHIBALD JAMES, 2 SQUADRON, RFC

The implications were far-reaching. Once the Royal Artillery had swallowed their pride and got used to taking fire orders from observers not under their direct control, the potential of air observation was obvious. Unseen indirect targets could be carefully registered by batteries, which could then hold themselves in readiness to open up a devastating fire as and when required. In particular, hostile German batteries, once identified, could be systematically targeted and eliminated as threats. The battlefield would never be the same again.

A British Kite balloon in the process of being inflated for artillery observation purposes. Kite balloons were instrumental in ranging shells directly onto enemy targets that could not be seen from the ground.

seconds it would take for those shells to arrive at the target. You then shifted the wing of your aeroplane to have an unrestricted view of the target and you saw the fall of the shell or shells. The system of correcting faults was this. You had imaginary circles drawn round the target, 25 yards, 50 yards, 150, 200, 250, 300, 350, 400 – and you had a simple letter and figure code to indicate two things: the clock-face point at which the shells were falling, in other words

The British kite balloons complemented the services provided by the aircraft. They had many advantages in that they could remain aloft all day and all night, the observers were not distracted by the responsibilities of flying an aircraft and had near perfect communication with the ground by telephones. This meant that if the German batteries suspended fire for the fear of discovery, as they often did when aircraft passed by, then

One of the best known British airfields used by the Royal Flying Corp in the Great War was Vert Galland wh the DH2s of 32 Squadron were based.

Germans killed by an accurate British artillery engagement.

taken aloft and by 1915 both sides had developed the first scout aircraft designed to shoot down the reconnaissance aircraft. Of course before they could do that efficiently the scouts first had to clear the skies of opposing scouts. Thus a battle for control of the skies developed and began to escalate in proportion to the importance of the prizes to be gained from unfettered observation. Unfortunately the scout pilots' role soon became so wreathed with glamour that then, and ever since, this allure has deflected attention from the 'real' role of the RFC.

In late 1915 the Germans gained the upper hand through the clear superiority of their Fokker E III monoplane scouts. This simple monoplane of limited performance had one great asset – a forward-firing machine gun that used an interrupter gear to allow it to pour bullets straight ahead without hitting the whirling propeller. Two young inspirational Fokker pilots, Leutnants Max Immelmann and Oswald Boelcke, set about honing the skills and tactics that would come to form the basics of aerial scout tactics. Intuitively utilizing the diving ability and forward firing strength of the Fokker, they sought to dive down from out of the glare of the sun, seeking surprise, only opening fire from close range and always looking for an easy kill with minimum risk to themselves. It was important not to

they would be almost permanently out of action. In general the balloons were best at reporting the overall situation and locating German batteries firing, but aircraft were far better at ranging the guns directly onto their targets.

SCOUTS – MASTERING A NEW TRADE

It soon became obvious that no army could allow enemy aircraft free access above their lines for the purpose of photographic reconnaissance and artillery observation. Soon the first machine guns were being

FOKKER E III MONO-WING FIGHTER

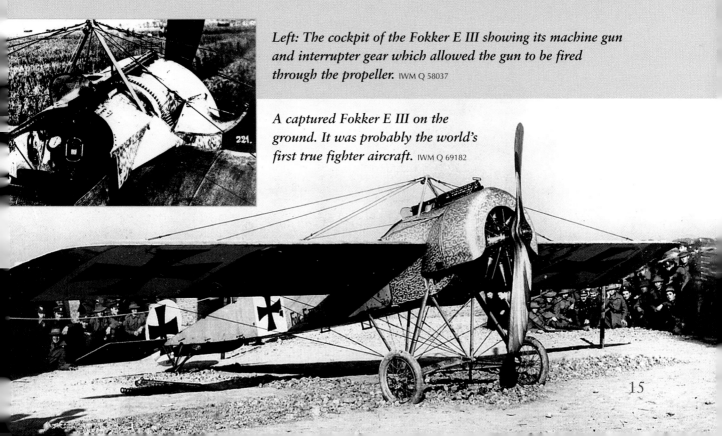

Left: The cockpit of the Fokker E III showing its machine gun and interrupter gear which allowed the gun to be fired through the propeller. IWM Q 58037

A captured Fokker E III on the ground. It was probably the world's first true fighter aircraft. IWM Q 69182

Max Immelmann. IWM Q 45328   *Oswald Boelcke.* IWM Q 63147

give a chance to their opponents; to kill before the victim had seen them was the ideal. One pass, then they would zoom away, before considering a second attack if it was necessary. As they mastered their new trade so their scores of 'victories' began to mount.

PLANS

On the ground the French and British were initially brashly confident that they would smash through the German trench lines. But they spent 1915 painfully trying to master the complex new language of modern industrial war. The trenches, the barbed wire, the machine guns, the huge destructive potential of massed artillery, the incredible numbers of mobilized men; they all combined together to pose new and intractable problems. Finally, in 1916, the industrial might and manpower of the Allies were properly harnessed to the task in hand. The Russians and Italians would launch co-ordinated offensives, but the pièce de resistance was to be a huge combined Franco-British effort on the Western Front intended to smash through the German line in the Somme sector. Unfortunately the Germans declined to lie back and simply await their fate, but took the initiative themselves by attacking the French at Verdun. The original Allied plans for a summer offensive in the Somme area were changed as it became obvious that the British would have

to take more of a leading role.

General Sir Douglas Haig planned to launch twenty-five of his divisions supported by some 1,500 guns and howitzers into the attack along a wide frontage of 25,000 yards to the north of the River Somme. The Fourth Army under the command of Lieutenant General Sir Henry Rawlinson was to be given the main role in the attack. It was considered that the artillery would suppress resistance and that the infantry would have little problem in opening up a wide gap in the German line. This the Germans would find impossible to plug with their reserves and the cavalry could then go through the centre to penetrate deep behind the lines. The final stage would see an advance to roll up the German line towards Arras.

SYMBIOTIC RELATIONSHIP

Before the RFC could get down to the business of preparing for the Somme Offensive of 1916, one way or another they would have to overcome the 'Fokker scourge', if they were to carry on providing the services the army required on a day-to-day basis. By this time aircraft had fully proved their military value to the High Command of the British Army. No longer an optional extra, they were fundamental to the business of winning the war on the ground, mainly through their symbiotic relationship with the guns. The army co-operation corps squadrons were charged with a series of onerous interlinked tasks: the provision of a comprehensive service of photographic reconnaissance and artillery observation; flying contact patrols during attacks; bombing raids to disrupt communications and harass the Germans in their rest billets. All this had to be

Lieutenant General Sir Henry Rawlinson.

General Sir Douglas Haig.

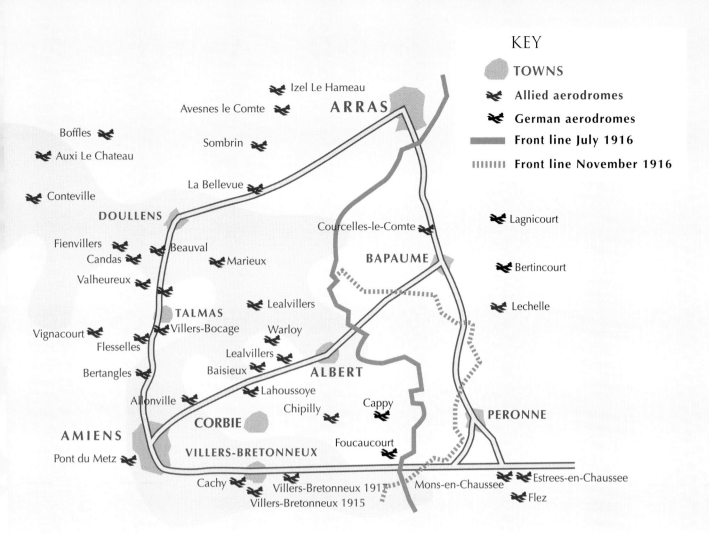

KEY

🛩 TOWNS
🛩 Allied aerodromes
🛩 German aerodromes
▬ Front line July 1916
⊪⊪ Front line November 1916

Izel Le Hameau
Avesnes le Comte
ARRAS
Boffles
Auxi Le Chateau
Sombrin
La Bellevue
Conteville
DOULLENS
Courcelles-le-Comte
Fienvillers
Beauval
BAPAUME
Candas
Marieux
Valheureux
Lealvillers
TALMAS
Villers-Bocage
Warloy
Vignacourt
Lealvillers
Flesselles
Baisieux
ALBERT
Bertangles
Lahoussoye
Allonville
Chipilly
Cappy
CORBIE
PERONNE
AMIENS
Foucaucourt
Pont du Metz
VILLERS-BRETONNEUX
Cachy
Villers-Bretonneux 1917
Mons-en-Chaussee
Estrees-en-Chaussee
Villers-Bretonneux 1915
Flez
Lagnicourt
Bertincourt
Lechelle

ALLIED & GERMAN AERODROMES IN THE SOMME AREA

achieved whilst at the same time beating back the German Air Force and thereby depriving the German Army of the same aerial facilities. In the face of the still potent Fokker threat in early 1916, truly Herculean efforts were demanded of the RFC and their army co-operation aircraft, the BE2 C, in the months leading up to the Battle of the Somme.

The BE2 C was totally unsuited to the job of course, it had the observer in front and the pilot behind, whereas with any sense, it should have been the pilot in front and the observer behind, but it wasn't! So the observer sat in a cockpit, with four struts very close each side of him, wires to brace him well in, and in front, none behind. And a little seat he could just get in to. And really he could do nothing at all except keep a look out. When it got at all hot and you

The BE2 C, the workhorse of the RFC in the first three years of the war. IWM Q 56847

'The BE2 C was totally unsuited to the job of course, it had the observer in front and the pilot behind... it should have been the pilot in front and the observer behind, but it wasn't!'

8300

were liable to be attacked from the tail as much as anywhere else, he simply had to get up on his seat, kneel on his seat, which was a jolly cold, drafty business at 8,000 feet even in the summer.

LIEUTENANT CECIL LEWIS, 9 SQUADRON, RFC

When the BE2 Cs were ordered in their thousands early in the war, no one had conceived of the necessity for anything other than a stable observation 'platform'. Now faced with the agile Fokkers they struggled to survive in the dangerous skies.

'ATTACK EVERYTHING'

The Battle of the Somme would be the first great test for the theories of aerial warfare being formulated by Brigadier General Hugh Trenchard who took command of the RFC in August 1915. Trenchard had already established a close working relationship with General Sir Douglas Haig; perhaps this was not surprising, for the two men had much in common. Both were less fluent in speech than on paper, both were utterly committed to the ultimate goal of victory, and both proved themselves willing to sacrifice lives where they considered it necessary for the greater good of their country. Trenchard, had developed a relentlessly offensive aerial strategy. It was a simple but effective concept of relentless scout patrols penetrating deep behind the German lines to beat back German aircraft and keep them as far as possible from the vital front line areas and accepting with equanimity the consequences of an occasional German aircraft breaking through to prey on the British army co-operation machines working above the trenches. Trenchard ordered his men to keep on flying over the line despite the 'Fokker scourge', his only compromise being that formations of aircraft were sent out on missions formerly carried out by lone aircraft to seek security in numbers. Nevertheless, underpinning everything was the principle that losses must be accepted to get the results required. The gamble worked and covered the cracks until the arrival of a new generation of British aircraft – the FE2 B, the DH2, the Nieuport Scout and the Sopwith 11/2 Strutter – which allowed the RFC to seize complete control of the skies above the Somme battlefield just at the time when it mattered most – in July 1916.

The FE2 Bs were two-seater, pusher aircraft with the engine behind the pilot. They performed a multi-purpose role

Brigadier General Hugh Trenchard.

German soldiers gather round the body of a dead airman who has fallen from his aircraft. This was a constant hazard for RFC observers who were perched high, unstrapped and without parachutes in their cockpits.

carrying out offensive patrols, reconnaissance flights and bombing missions. They were a sturdy aircraft, not overly fast but difficult to shoot down.

Went on reconnaissance. Unfortunately the camera jammed. Five Fokkers hung on our tails but did not close in to fighting range. The wind was strong against us coming back. We were lucky not to have another running fight. Perhaps they realised we carry a sting in our tail. These running fights are the devil. It is annoying to have to be passive resisters, caring only about the Reconnaissance and getting back with the report and the photos.

CAPTAIN HAROLD WYLLIE, 23 SQUADRON, RFC

The FE2 B pilots found that the best method of defence was to circle round to protect each other's vulnerable tail from the lurking Fokkers. A second Lewis gun was fitted on a telescopic mounting between the two cockpits. To use it the observer was required to stand on his seat and fire the Lewis backwards over pilot and the upper wing to partially cover the blind spot to the rear. Perched as he was with only his feet and ankles actually within the cockpit, the observer was almost completely exposed and could easily fall out to his inevitable death in the days before parachutes.

The British FE2 B. IWM Q 63183

The other key British aircraft to make its debut early in 1916 was the DH2. A single-seater, pusher fighter of slightly comical appearance it, more than any other aircraft perhaps, was instrumental in winning domination of the Somme skies.

If a Hun sees a De Hav he runs for his life; they won't come near them. It was only yesterday that one of the fellows came across a Fokker. The Fokker dived followed by the De Hav but the wretched Fokker dived so hard that when he tried to pull his machine out his elevator broke and he dived into our Lines; not a shot was fired.

SECOND LIEUTENANT GWILYM LEWIS, 32 SQUADRON, RFC

Major Lanoe Hawker V.C. who commanded the first squadron of DH2s soon developed his tactical thinking to a peak of sophistication that encapsulated both his personality and the abiding ethos of the RFC. 'Tactical Orders by Officer Commanding No. 24 Squadron, Royal Flying Corps: "ATTACK EVERYTHING."

Major Lanoe Hawker V.C.

BRITISH AIRCO DH2 - SINGLE SEAT PUSHER FIGHTER

Left: The DH2 was to make its debut in the early part of 1916. Though a small and comical looking fighter, it was strongly built and able to absorb alot of punishment. The DH2 was instrumental in winning back the skies for the British. IWM Q 67534

Right: A rear view photograph shows the rotary 100hp Le Rhône engine which could generate 85mph at 7,000 feet and 77mph at 10,000 feet. IWM Q 67534

WITNESSES TO TRAGEDY

For the coming offensive the RFC concentrated some 185 aircraft in the Somme area, plus the outside aircraft flying on bombing missions. Of these some seventy-six were the new scout aircraft. The French had also concentrated considerable aircraft for the offensive. To face this aerial Armada the Germans could only deploy some 129 aircraft of which only a meagre nineteen were scouts. As the British concentrated all their resources for the offensive the Germans were hampered by their equally onerous commitments battling the French Air Service over Verdun. The Allies had achieved a significant aerial superiority over the Somme as the Fokker menace spluttered out ignominiously – symbolized by the death of the great Fokker ace Max Immelmann in late June.

In retrospect, it is obvious that the British were not really ready to go 'over the top' on 1st July 1916. Their artillery bombardment may have been impressive to watch, but the length and depth of the front attacked meant that the actual number of shells falling on any given area of ground was nowhere near the concentration required to destroy the barbed wire and defences. Furthermore, modern artillery tactics were still in their infancy and there was no sophistication in their bombardment techniques. Crudely timed 'lifts' meant that shells ceased falling on the German front line trenches at the very moment that the British infantry made their advance across No Man's Land. The use of true 'creeping' barrages, lines of bursting shells advancing just in front of the attacking troops, was then only at the experimental stage of development. There was no real idea of using defensive 'curtains' of fire to break up

> The German counter-bombardment severed telephone links, killed runners and the advancing waves disappeared into the unknown.

and destroy German counter-attacks. Insufficient guns had been assigned to the destruction of the identified German batteries which in consequence survived largely unscathed, ready to open up on the British infantry in their assembly trenches and No Man's Land when the moment came. Indeed as a more general point most of the British gunners simply did not have the skills or training to carry out such complex fire plans with the requisite degree of speed and accuracy. As to the infantry tactics they were so simple that they hardly justified such a designation. The soldiers who went 'over the top' were mostly the inexperienced volunteers of 'Kitchener's Army' and it was generally considered that their best chance of retaining their cohesion in crossing No Man's Land under fire was to advance in long waves at a steady walking pace.

So it was that on 1st July the RFC contact patrols witnessed tragedy unparalleled in British military history before or since. It was their role to determine the exact progress of troops on the ground. This information was vital to inform the supporting artillery batteries, as it

The Morane Parasol. IWM Q 55974

The Tyneside Irish walk steadily towards the village of La Boisselle and into a hail of bullets. The village was occ by the Germans on 1st July 1916, a day which was to witness the greatest disaster in British military history.

had been found through bitter experience that conventional means of communication frequently broke down when the troops launched themselves across No Man's Land. The German counter-bombardment severed telephone links, killed runners and the advancing waves disappeared into the unknown. As Lieutenant Cecil Lewis flew his Morane Parasol above La Boisselle his eyes were glued to the ground.

We went right down to 3,000 feet to see what was happening. We had a klaxon horn on the undercarriage of the Morane – a great big 12-volt klaxon and I had a button which I used to press out a letter to tell the infantry that we wanted to know where they were. When they heard us hawking at them from above, they had little red Bengal flares, they carried them in their pockets, they would put a match to their flares. All along the line wherever there was a chap there would be a flare and we would note these flares down on the map and Bob's your uncle! It was one thing to practise this but quite another thing for them to really do it when they were under fire and particularly when things began to go a bit badly. Then they jolly well wouldn't light anything and small blame to them because it drew the fire of the enemy on to them at once. So we went down looking for flares and we only got about two flares on the whole front. We were bitterly disappointed.

SECOND LIEUTENANT CECIL LEWIS, 3 SQUADRON, RFC

'...the enemy's aircraft inspired our troops with a feeling of defencelessness against the enemy's mastery of the air.'

possible jumping-off point for the next major attacks. This would make the main assault a lot easier and hopefully reduce the overall toll of casualties. In all this fighting the RFC continued to play its part. It was absolutely central to the detailed planning of the attacks for the contact patrols to determine where the troops had got to, while the aerial photography exposed the exact location of hitherto unseen trench lines, machine-gun posts and trench mortars. The pilots and observer of the RFC were worked to the limits of their physical and mental limits. Understandably some began to crack under the strain.

The heat of the long summer days was terrific, and our flying hours were many. All these facts assisted to play upon the temperaments of those who were flying in France for the first time, and had not got confidence either in their ability or in their aeroplanes. I can remember my bedroom companion in the farmhouse in which we were billeted, felt as I did, and how each of us lay awake in the darkness, not telling the other that sleep would not come, listening to the incessant roar of the guns, and thinking of the dawn patrol next morning. At last we could bear it no longer, and calling out to each other admitted a mutual feeling of terror and foreboding. We lit the candles to hide the dark, and after that felt a bit better, and somehow got through that night as we had to get through the next day.

SECOND LIEUTENANT HAROLD BALFOUR, 60 SQUADRON, RFC

LIMITS OF ENDURANCE

The offensive carried on regardless; it had to, this was no isolated battle but the major Allied offensive of 1916 and a key component of their overall Grand Strategy. The pattern of fighting which had been established in mid-July, continued right through August: desperate attacks by just a few British battalions to gain some tactically significant feature, their desperate efforts to consolidate any gains and the equally determined German counter-attacks. Names that even now cause a shiver of communal recognition were at the centre of these battles: Delville Wood, Longueval, Trones Wood, Ovillers, High Wood and Pozières. These battles have since been cruelly satirized as nothing more than the deaths of thousands of men in futile attempts to move their general's cocktail cabinet a few yards nearer to Berlin. But in fact the aim was simple – to gain the best

Yet it was worth all the pain. The aerial domination allowed the Royal Artillery to slowly get a grip on the battlefield. The German High Command was all too aware of the situation.

The beginning and the first weeks of the Somme battle were marked by a complete inferiority of our own air forces. The enemy's aeroplanes enjoyed complete freedom in carrying out distant reconnaissances. With the aid of aeroplane observation, the hostile artillery neutralized our guns and was able to range with the most extreme accuracy on the trenches occupied by our infantry; the required data for this was provided by undisturbed trench reconnaissance and photography. By means of bombing and machine-gun attacks from a low height against infantry, battery positions and marching columns, the enemy's aircraft inspired our troops with a feeling of defencelessness against the enemy's mastery of the air. On the other hand, our own aeroplanes only succeeded in quite exceptional cases in breaking through the hostile patrol barrage and carrying out distant reconnaissances; our artillery machines were driven off whenever they attempted to carry out registration for their own batteries. Photographic reconnaissance could not fulfil the demands made upon it. Thus, at decisive moments, the infantry frequently lacked the support of the German artillery either in counter-battery work or in barrage on the enemy's infantry massing for attack.

GENERAL FRITZ VON BELOW, HEADQUARTERS GERMAN FIRST ARMY

ICON

During the summer and autumn of 1916, one British scout pilot protecting the vital army co-operation aircraft began to emerge as a key personality – this was the iconic figure of Second Lieutenant Albert Ball who flew the French single-seater Nieuport 16 Scout. This was a streamlined tractor biplane which was superior in every respect to the Fokker with the sole exception of armament – the only firepower was a fixed forward firing Lewis gun mounted above the wing centre section and fired by a wire grip on the joystick. Again like the 'pushers' this dodged the central requirement for a synchronized gun firing through the propeller – this time

Second Lieutenant Albert Ball V.C.

A staged photograph of how a dog fight might have appeared.

by directing its fire above the span of the propeller. Ball took to flying ceaseless patrols across the German lines seeking out trouble wherever he could find it. He became the epitome of the RFC offensive spirit and no odds were too great for him to cock a snook at. On 22nd August, Ball took off as an escort to an FE2 B bombing mission. He ran into a large formation of German aircraft.

Met 12 Huns. No. 1 fight. I attacked and fired two drums, bringing the machine down just outside a village. All crashed up. No. 2 fight. I attacked and got under machine, putting in two drums. Hun went down in flames. No. 3 fight. I attacked and put in one drum. Machine went down and crashed on a housetop. All these fights were seen and reported by other machines that saw them go down. I only got hit 11 times in the planes, so I returned and got more ammunition. This time luck was not all on the spot. I was met by about 14 Huns, about 15 miles over their side. My windscreen was hit in four places, mirror broken, the spar of the left plane broken, also engine ran out of petrol. But I had good sport and good luck, but only just, for I was brought down about one mile over our side.

LIEUTENANT ALBERT BALL, 11 SQUADRON, RFC

It seemed that he could fly into a hail of bullets time and time again, to emerge with his aircraft shot to pieces but he himself unscathed. But his individualized tactics were beyond duplication by pilots who lacked his skills and suicidal bravery and could not duplicate the 'berserker' approach. Fighting the way he did, it was just a matter of time before he was killed. And yet for the moment he went from victory to victory. When Albert Ball eventually returned to England in October 1916 he had claimed some thirty-one victories.

BLOOD, SWEAT AND TEARS

British efforts towards the end of the summer were increasingly dominated by the preparations for the next major attack planned to take place on 15th September. The continuous small scale attacks over the previous two months had moved the British line forward less than a mile, on a front just three miles wide, at a cost of some 82,000 casualties – which was in itself worse than the results achieved on 1st July. Now there was to be another all-out assault fully utilizing the new techniques of more concentrated artillery bombardment and increasingly sophisticated use of creeping and standing barrages. The intention was a decisive breakthrough to exploit the painful 'wearing out' process. Once again reconnaissance and artillery observation was at a premium. Everything had to be risked to save the lives of thousands of infantrymen.

The Battle of Flers-Courcelette launched on 15th September 1916, was intended to capture the line from Morval to Le Sars. The blood, sweat and tears of the previous two months had achieved a start line close enough to the old German Third Line to offer some chance of success, but of course the Germans had not been idle. There were no longer open 'green fields' behind the Third Line; it was just the first in a series of three more fully-fledged trench systems. However, this time, Haig and Rawlinson were about to unveil a secret weapon – the tank – that offered them some hope of loosening the strangulating grip of trench warfare. The early tanks were slow, prone to breakdown at the drop of a hat and of course none of their crews had battle experience in their new ironclads. Rawlinson saw them not as a weapon of breakthrough, but one that would speed up the overall pace of the advance and thus keep up the whole momentum that was so important to Haig.

When the infantry and tanks went over the top, once again, Lieutenant Cecil Lewis was up on contact patrol at the vital moment.

> There was a half hour hurricane bombardment and then the tanks were put over. From the air at about 5 or 6,000 feet behind the lines watching this whole scene, there was this solid

Haig and Rawlinson's secret weapon, the tank, which offered hope in breaking the 'stalemate' on the Western Front.

> grey wool carpet of shell bursts, but it was just as if somebody had taken his finger in the snow and pulled it through the snow and left a sort of ribbon. There were four or five of these ribbons between Fricourt and Boisselle, and running back toward High Wood. Through these lanes at Zero Hour we saw the tanks beginning to lumber. They'd been cleared for the tanks to come in file. They came up three or four in file, one behind the other. Of course they were utterly unexpected, the first lot went sailing over the trenches and we thought, 'Well this is fine!' Because the whole thing was the year was getting a bit late, 'If we don't get through now, we never shall!' This was the great opportunity and hope was high. We thought, 'If they can get through the third line defences, we can put the cavalry through and the whole war will become mobile again!' And so we watched pretty carefully to see how things went. By this time all this area had been shelled for the best part of three months and it was contiguous shell holes for miles and miles. The ground looked from above like a pock-marked skin. All the trees had been shot, there was no greenery, there was nothing. Except amongst the grey wool of shell burst these lumbering chaps. One or two of them with

Ironclads leading the British advance. The tank was not viewed primarily as a weapon of breakthrough but rather to add extra momentum to an offensive.

red petrol tanks on their back; one even with a little mascot, a little fox terrier running behind the tank. Then one would stop and we had no idea why. Obviously it had been hit, or somebody had thrown a grenade at it, or it had a breakdown. At the end of two hours they had moved about a mile and we thought everything was going well and we came back because our petrol was finished.

LIEUTENANT CECIL LEWIS, 3 SQUADRON, RFC

On the ground there were still problems with surviving German machine guns, especially in those shell free 'lanes' so visible from the air. The infantry were left badly exposed when the tanks broke down or were held up, as was frequently the case. The German artillery fire also crashed out to flay the British jumping-off positions and to catch the infantry in the wastes of No Man's Land. However successful the RFC had been in directing counter-battery fire, it was self-evident that there were still not enough British guns being devoted to this most essential of tasks. It was not so much that either the RFC or Royal Artillery had failed; rather that the whole gargantuan scale of the counter-battery question had not yet been fully grasped. The consequence was serious casualties – nearly 30,000 in total. Nevertheless, the German front line positions were seized all along the 9,000 yard front and 4,500 yards of their new 'Second Line' was also lost near the village of Flers where the tanks had performed well. This, it should be noted, was the exception to the rule as many of the tanks suffered mechanical breakdowns. The German line had been

bent, bashed, reshaped and bitten into – but it retained its overall integrity. The morale of the defending troops was dented, but it endured; German manpower reserves were stretched, but still the reserve divisions moved forward to obstruct, halt and counter-attack to once more hold the British advance.

GERMAN AERIAL RENAISSANCE

During the battle the RFC broke new records for the amount of hours flown and the intensity of the aerial fighting: the contact patrols, artillery observation work, deep searching reconnaissance patrols, bombing raids – all covered by the aggressive posture of the scouts seeking out their prey. Yet the aerial operations in mid-September marked the median point before the pendulum of aerial warfare swung decisively back towards the Germans. The German aerial renaissance was triggered by the return to the Western Front of the incomparable Oswald Boelcke accompanied by his new scout squadron Jasta 2. They were equipped with the new Albatros DI scout.

A haggard Boelcke in the cockpit of his Albatros. This was to be the last photograph ever taken of him before his death.

This was the first scout to be armed with twin Spandau machine guns firing through the propeller without a corresponding loss in aerial performance, due to its careful streamlining and the awesome power of its Mercedes engine which took it up to speeds of nearly 110mph. One of the new pilots flying with Boelcke was Leutnant Manfred von Richthofen. Born in 1892, of an aristocratic family, Richthofen had a keen interest in hunting which he was soon to take

GERMAN ALBATROS D I - JASTA 2

SPECIFICATIONS

Manufacturer: Albatros Werke GmbH
Type: Fighter
Engine: Mercedes D.III, 160 hp
Max Speed: 115-120 mph

Ceiling: 17,000 ft
Endurance: 1.5 hours
Crew: 1
Armament: 2 machine guns

to new heights. Early in the war he served as a cavalryman before a desire for excitement caused him to gravitate into the German Air Service. His first victory occurred on 17th September when he shot down an FE2 B crewed by the veterans Lieutenant Lionel Morris and Lieutenant Tom Rees. They had simply had no chance. Although Richthofen was still raw as a scout pilot, his Albatros so totally outclassed the FE2 B it gave him a margin of error that more than compensated for any lack of combat skills.

Trenchard was quickly alive to the new threat posed by the Albatros, but was determined that the RFC would continue to do its duty. The RFC still had a considerable numerical superiority and the Germans still rarely crossed the British front line, so they were automatically on the back foot as far as reconnaissance and artillery observation was concerned. Trenchard was not the type of man to bend with the wind – he stood firm and he pushed back.

BLOOD SACRIFICE

Whatever the tactical gains and theoretical advances made in the September attacks, one thing remained clear. The British were as far from a strategic breakthrough as ever. The Fourth Army had carried the original German Third Line system after three months of intensive fighting; but they now faced yet another trench system built by the Germans along the ridge stretching from Le Transloy to Thilloy, whilst two more trench systems were under construction stretching back towards Bapaume and beyond. The Reserve Army on top of Thiepval Ridge still faced multiple German trench lines,

Leutnant Manfred von Richthofen.

bolstered by the all too familiar fortified woods and villages. Yet, Haig was convinced that the German Army was ready to collapse. Intelligence reports had indicated problems of morale amongst the hard-pressed German infantry and Haig was determined to carry on the offensive. The decision having been taken, the British Army continued to batter against the German lines. When the weather broke in October the infantry and artillery were hamstrung by the mud and it was extremely difficult for the RFC to carry out its duties. Indeed, it was often just too wet and windy to fly at all. When they could get airborne they were harried by the new Albatros scouts, although they still continued to fly their missions and carry out the vital army co-operation duties. The only silver lining for the RFC was the death of Oswald Boelcke in an accidental mid-air collision on 28th October 1916.

Oswald Boelcke had proved a truly great mentor to his young pilots, leading from the front to achieve some forty 'victories' on his own account. Inspired by his example, many like Richthofen began to score regular victories as they discovered that the British had nothing to compare with the sheer power of the Albatros DI or the slightly modified Albatros DIIs which were also beginning to be delivered to the Jastas. The death of Boelcke was a tragedy for the German Air Service. Yet in one sense the work of their young master – Boelcke was just twenty-five years old when he died – was done. Jasta 2 had learnt well and Richthofen, who had already shot down six aircraft, would soon take on his mantle.

The Albatros scouts continued to

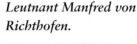

MANFRED VON RICTHOFEN'S ALBATROS D. V

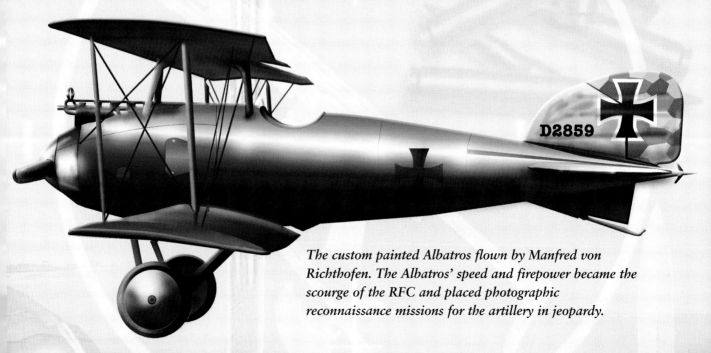

D2859

The custom painted Albatros flown by Manfred von Richthofen. The Albatros' speed and firepower became the scourge of the RFC and placed photographic reconnaissance missions for the artillery in jeopardy.

Germany says farewell to its hero. Boelcke is buried with full military honours. IWM Q 73532

TO THE MEMORY OF CAPTAIN
BOELKE, OUR BRAVE AND CHIVALROUS
OPPONENT.

FROM, THE ENGLISH
ROYAL FLYING CORPS.

The RFC recognized the death of Boelc
This message attached to a wreath, wa
dropped by Lieutenant Thomas Green
3 Squadron who risked his life deliveri
it over the German lines.

extract an increasingly painful blood sacrifice as the Somme offensive dragged on into the late autumn. Other new German single-seater scouts arriving on the scene in late 1916, such as the Halberstadt DII, the Roland DII and the Pfalz DII, which were all perfectly good scout aircraft, but all overshadowed by the dramatic success of the Albatros DI and DIIs. Yet, although the casualties rose sharply, the RFC managed to continue delivering the services that Haig required right to the bitter end of the Somme. Whenever the weather broke for long enough to allow the aircraft to get aloft, up they would duly go. One of the great lessons of aerial warfare had been learnt. Supremacy in the air meant the ability to keep army photographic reconnaissance and artillery observation aircraft above the front and the question of casualties incurred in doing so was almost immaterial in comparison.

COMING OF AGE

On 13th November, the Battle of the Ancre was launched as the last gasp of the Somme Offensive. General Sir Hubert Gough's relatively fresh Fifth Army lunged forward into the valley of the River Ancre to the north of the Somme. Assisted by a reasonably effective artillery bombardment, the infantry made considerable initial progress. Beaumont Hamel fell at last, Beaucourt was captured and the positions on the Thiepval Ridge further developed. However, the attack on the Serre and Redan Ridges further north failed. The attacks continued for a few days, but as the weather worsened it became obvious that nothing more of real value would be achieved. And so, at last, on 18th November, Haig suspended the attacks – the agony that was the Battle of the Somme was over.

In the end the swing of the technological pendulum had left the RFC in a position of marked inferiority. It was obvious that the FE2 Bs and the DH2s had had their day. The use of pusher aircraft to overcome the lack of an effective machine-gun synchronization mechanism had been a temporarily successful stratagem, but now more powerful and faster tractor aircraft like the

Albatros were dominating the skies. But overall for the RFC, the Battle of the Somme marked the point where it finally came of age as a fighting service. The battle had been almost entirely fought over and behind the German lines and the RFC had successfully carried out the role in the face of a skilful, well-equipped opposition. The aces may have got the glory but the army co-operation pilots and observers in their totally obsolescent BE2 Cs were the real heroes whose efforts saved the lives of thousands of British soldiers just as they killed countless Germans. Of the 583 RFC casualties suffered on the Western Front between June and December 1916 the majority were over the Somme battlefields. But in the tragic ledger of the Somme, the losses they suffered have to be offset against the enormous value of their work. For the RFC at least it was 'Somme Success'. Next it would be 'Up the Arras' in the Bloody April of 1917.

THE COMPLETE STORY OF THE SOMME

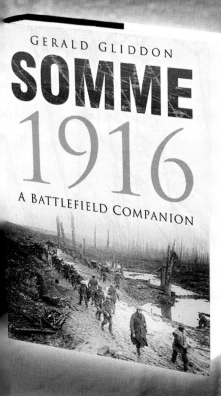
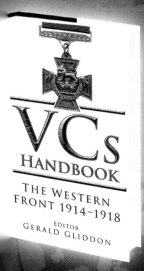
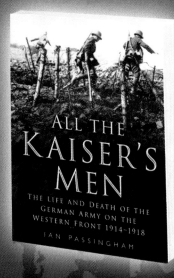

'Two years in the making.
Ten minutes in the destroying.
That was our history.'

JOHN HARRIS -
FROM HIS NOVEL
COVENANT WITH DEATH.

28

THE BATTLE OF THE SOMME 2ND JULY-18TH NOVEMBER 1916

For almost everyone who has heard of the Battle of the Somme it is famous for the terrible losses on the First Day and the tactics that were used. To raise objections such as the fact that British losses were greater on a per diem basis in the German Spring Offensive of 1918, the Advance to Victory in 1918 and the Battle of Arras in 1917; or, perhaps more pertinently, that the Battle lasted for four and a half months, not one day, is to confuse the issue with facts.

By Revd. Nigel Cave - Editor of the Battleground Europe series.

This article was extracted from *Battlefields Review*. Nigel Cave has written several books on the Battle of the Somme: *Serre, Gommecourt, Beaumont Hamel, Delville Wood*, all of which have been published by Pen & Sword Books Ltd.

D**espite** these observations on the fixation with 1st July 1916, it is only reasonable to understand why 1st July could have become a fixture in the collective British memory. It did witness the destruction of the Pals ideal, itself a peculiarly British phenomenon. For, with recruitment coming from very small geographical areas and close-knit communities, a bad day for a Pals battalion would have dire consequences in its recruitment area.

Thus the losses of the Tyneside Irish and Tyneside Scottish brigades at La Boiselle devastated Newcastle; the losses of Barnsley, Accrington, Sheffield, Leeds and Bradford Pals in the Serre area, caused intense grief throughout these Yorkshire and Lancashire towns and cities – and so the list goes on. The fact that it was the worst day of the war thus far, for practically all the battalions that went over the top (and so many of them were Pals battalions) on that day, adds to the poignancy. John Harris, in his memorable novel, *Covenant with Death*, ends his fictional account of his hero's war service in a Pals battalion (loosely base on the Sheffield City Battalion), that culminates on 1st July at Serre, as follows:

Two years in the making. Ten minutes in the destroying. That was our history.

With the loss of many of the original members of these battalions, there was also a loss of naivety, an awareness of 'the reality of war' – what some have described as 'the loss of innocence' – an unhappy epitaph for the Pals ideal born in the early days of the conflict. It was an epitaph, because although all of the battalions were rebuilt, they never were to have the same characteristics of those first years of the war. For these reasons it is easy to understand the concern with the 'First Day of the Somme'. It was the British introduction of the first land war in their history to include mass numbers of their people. They could now join that club which included all

CASUALTIES ON THE FIRST DAY

The British had 165,000 casualties in the first eleven days of the German Spring Offensive, which commenced on 21st March 1918. The army's greatest one day disaster in terms of casualties, was the surrender of Singapore (85,000 – of whom a huge number were to die as PoWs).

BRITISH OFFICERS	BRITISH OTHER RANKS
Killed/died of wounds - 993	Killed/died of wounds - 18,247
Wounded - 1,337	Wounded - 34,156
Missing - 96	Missing - 2,056
Prisoners - 12	Prisoners - 573
TOTAL - 2,438	TOTAL - 55,032

BRITISH TOTAL

Killed/died of wounds - 19,240
Wounded - 35,156
Missing -2,152
Prisoners - 585

TOTAL - 57,470

The German casualties are something of a guesstimate because of the method of casualty returns. A figure broadly accepted is 8,000 of whom 2,200 were prisoners. It has been suggested that the German figure is somewhat understated but only by a thousand or two – certainly nowhere near the British losses which were in the order of at least six British to one German.

the other major powers – the Americans during the Civil War; the Japanese in the Russo-Japanese War; and the actions of 1914, for example, merely added to the bloody military experience of France, Germany and Austro-Hungary. It was a rude welcome to the nature of modern continental warfare.

But the Battle of the Somme, as mentioned above, was a battle that went on for another 140 days. Officially, it is known as the Battles of the Somme, 1916 – this included twelve individual battles and three actions. These are as follows:

BATTLE OF ALBERT 1916
1st - 13th July

ATTACK ON THE GOMMECOURT SALIENT
1st July

BATTLE OF BAZENTIN
14th - 17th July

ATTACK AT FROMELLES (AUBERS RIDGE)
19th July

ATTACKS ON HIGH WOOD
20th - 25th July

BATTLE OF DELVILLE WOOD
15th July - 3rd September

BATTLE OF POZIÈRES
23rd July – 3rd - 6th September

BATTLE OF GINCHY
9th September

BATTLE OF FLERS-COURCELETTE
15th - 22nd September

BATTLE OF THIEPVAL
26th - 28th September

BATTLE OF LE TRANSLOY
1st - 8th October

BATTLE OF ANCRE HEIGHTS
1st October – 13th-18th November

The official record has twenty-four British divisions in action (or in the theatre of action) on 1st July 1916, though about a third of these took no part in the fighting (which is not to say that they did not suffer casualties, if only from long distance shelling). By the end of the fighting fifty-four divisions and two cavalry divisions had been engaged – almost the entire fighting capacity of the BEF. Some of these formations had been in several of the battles that composed the Somme, 1916. Thus the 18th (Eastern) Division was engaged six times; the 56th (London) five times, as also the 20th (Light). The Canadian 1st, 2nd and 3rd Divisions were engaged three times. Whilst the Australian 1st and 2nd Divisions are only listed once (as is also, for example, the 63rd (Royal Naval Division), this does not reflect either on their contribution to the battle nor their casualties at Pozières and the Battle of the Ancre respectively.

These long lists show that there was more in time and manpower and human suffering that the popular perception of a battle that seemingly lasted one day. But there are other matters to consider as well.

The general memory of the Great War is of lines of men climbing out of their trenches and setting off in almost parade like fashion to attack the enemy in the distance, invariably safely ensconced in positions on top of a hill and under a hail of lethal machine-gun fire. Whilst this is true in a number of cases, rather closer examination shows that there were a variety of tactics used in the advance. For example, the 1st Newfoundland Regiment adopted a procedure of advancing in either file or single file – also used by the neighbouring 36th (Ulster) Division. For those men in the second or third wave it was almost impossible to advance in line, as they had first to come through the gaps in the British wire and were then faced with a mass of shell holes. When it comes down to it, every infantry battle involves leaving trenches or protective areas and advancing on the enemy. But certainly, there is much to criticize – inadequate or poor artillery support; inflexible planning down to the individual soldier (a consequence of a lack of realistic training, a chronic shortage of battle-hardened NCOs and junior officers and staff officers – and battle experience); unrealistic expectations; over-estimation of the impact of the artillery pounding on the German lines; under-estimation of the newly refurbished German defences between Gommecourt and Fricourt; and an under-estimation of the German soldier. But by concentrating on the First Day an appreciation of the ability of the army to adapt to the realities so cruelly exposed to it has been lost.

A famous Somme image showing British soldiers advancing orderly into No Man's Land.

The introduction of the tank at Flers-Courcelette was to open a new chapter in trench warfare. Unreliable as they were, Douglas Haig was to order large numbers of them.

During the Battle of the Somme, lessons were learnt. The dawn attack on 14th July was a masterstroke, a feat which the French, at least, considered to be impossible. Their incredulity was due to the fact that by mid-1916 the French concentrated on artillery as their major offensive weapon, with the infantry used more cautiously than in the heady days of August 1914. The British had plenty of infantry but relatively few of the essential heavy guns: by November 1916, Haig had almost 65 per cent more heavy guns available than he had on 1st July.

Shell quality was poor; there were as yet no smoke shells available (smoke fired by mortar was a poor and inadequate substitute) and there was no instantaneous fuze. The creeping barrage was developed, but all artillery work depended upon both good observation and book communications. These Chinese Barrages – an intensification of barrage fire to trick the enemy to think that an attack was imminent and thus draw them from their dugouts and shelters – was adopted to reasonable effect.

Co-ordination between the arms improved as the battle progressed, though this is not to suggest that things were perfect: far from it. Brigadier General Tudor's fire plan for the 9th (Scottish) Division on 14th July was an excellent example of what could be achieved. As the days dragged on, the battle performance of all elements and ranks significantly improved: experience learnt on the battlefield. As the Official History notes:

Yet natural leaders there were in plenty, and the gallantry and spirit of officers and men were beyond all praise; the pity of it was that they should have had to learn their business in the hard school of the Somme.

In September 1916 the tank made its first appearance on the battlefield at Flers-Courcelette. There were far too few of them and they were unreliable machines. But it opened a new chapter in warfare, and Douglas Haig was an enthusiast, ordering an immense number afterwards; even though many in the army – not least some infantry men – had doubts about their value.

The role of the machine-gun, heavy and light, continued to be adapted and refined: though it is interesting to note that even before 1st July the Fourth Army, in its tactical notes, recommended that the Lewis gun should be regarded as an automatic rifle. Lessons were learnt not only by gunners and infantry but also by the other composite parts of the British army, from signalling operations to the medical services.

And, of course, if the British learnt much about warfare during the Somme, so did the Germans. Germany had been bruised by the fighting at Verdun, her last great offensive on the Western Front before the onslaught of Spring 1918. Ludendorff noted in his memoirs that at the end of the fighting in 1916: *The German army had been fought to a standstill and was utterly worn out*; whilst Hindenburg, in the conference on 9th January 1917 which approved the unrestricted U-Boat campaign, stated:

We must save the men from a second Somme battle. Hans Grote wrote in *Somme: in its results the first material-battle of the World War turned to the disadvantage of the victorious Germans, for no art of the commander could give them back the trained soldiery which had been destroyed.*

As a result of their lessons learnt, the Germans issued a new doctrine for the defensive battle in December 1916, based on an active and elastic defence. This was supported by a manual compiled by General von Bulow (commanding First Army) and his Chief of Staff, Colonel von Lossberg. The decision was also taken to withdraw to the fortified and in-depth defences of the Hindenburg Line.

The Somme was the start of an almost incessant series of major engagements for the British army, which only ended with the Armistice in November 1918. It marked the coming of age of the British as a major military player on the continent of Europe.

The literature on the Somme continues to grow at a staggering rate. Military History as an academic discipline has suffered, at least in the Anglo-Saxon world, in recent years: it seems imperative to show the sociological relevance and to downplay the 'art of war'. A liberal aversion to warfare will not help it go away, most regrettably. This aside, there has been a good range of books on the battle which has moved the discussion forward. This is an important development as a number of authorities have observed, the progress (or lack of it) of the 'fighting methods' of the British army have been inextricably tangled with the wrangling over the reputation of Sir Douglas Haig. Notable amongst these works is *Command on the Western Front*, by Robin

Prior and Trevor Wilson. This book examines the career of Sir Henry Rawlinson as a commander, and devotes some 100 pages to his performance as commander of the Fourth Army at the Somme. It follows on from the work of men like Tim Travers, who produced new direction to the discussion. The fighting after 1st July has now got to a range of titles that examine particular phases – one thinks of Terry Norman's *The Hell They Called High Wood*; of Colin Hughes's *Mametz* and Peter Charlton's *Pozières*; and of the outstanding (and masterly) *The Tanks at Flers* by Trevor Pigeon. Peter Liddle has produced the useful *The 1916 Battle of the Somme – A Reappraisal*. Martin Middlebrook wrote the first (and possibly the best) of the personal accounts: his *First Day of the Somme* has become a classic.

The *Battleground Europe* series now boasts twelve detailed books on small parts of the battle area, with another half dozen or so to come. New biographies, such as those on Ivor Maxse (*Far from a Donkey*, John Baynes) and Brigadier General AM Asquith (*Command in the Royal Naval Division* by Christopher Page) and the reprint of Great War classics – *Twelve Days* by Sydney Rogerson and the *War Diaries of the Master of Belhaven*, for example, helps to increase the accessibility of a broader range of material to a wider audience. The recent reprinting of the entire *Official History* means that more people can judge the much-maligned work from a personal reading. Flawed as it most certainly is, this is a most important source work. It is also pleasing to note the reprinting of a number of divisional histories: uneven in quality though these are, some of them are outstandingly good, amongst them those of the 2nd, 8th, 9th, 15th and 18th Divisions.

There are, of course, glaring gaps: most obviously accessible works about the German and French contributions. This lack has resulted in a natural tendency to engage in national navel-gazing. We have tended, perforce, to study the war from an almost entirely British perspective. Work on the German archives for units and formations at Vimy and Beaumont Hamel by Norbert Krüger, for example, has shown that far more of the German archives have survived the Second World War than many had thought. Certainly

there is a great need to bring some balance from these sources to our understanding of the Somme.

The Somme battlefield attracts the British (and, increasingly, Canadians and Australians) by the thousand. It is in attractive, rolling countryside. The Commonwealth cemeteries scattered over its area act as signposts to actions and at the same time serve to bring battle down to the level of the individual tragedy. I would suggest that we do not serve the men of 1916 well if we continue to fix our sights exclusively on the disaster and the tactical errors that were the First Day of the Somme. We should also look at the later battle which, after all, produced another 390,000 or so British casualties. And let us not forget the French – 150,000 casualties – and the Germans, who probably suffered a casualty list somewhere near the total British and French casualty lists combined.

FOOTNOTE

The Germans used some ninety-six divisions (Official History, 1916: Vol II, p.555), but it should be borne in mind that their divisions were smaller numerically than their British counterparts and, of course, they also faced the French divisions involved in the southern part of the battlefield.

A British division at the First Day of the Battle of the Somme would have consisted of about 18,500 men. It would have about 10,000 rifles, 204 machine guns, forty trench mortars and sixty-four guns under command. As the battle progressed the number of rifles (or bayonets, as they were sometimes called) would have diminished because of casualties and the time gap in getting drafts. Battalions could be reduced from about 1,100 men to 400 or so for periods of time.

A German division on the First Day had nine battalions (compared with the British twelve) and each battalion had about 800 men. The German divisions on the Somme were all at full strength and had had relatively little fighting since the early days of the war. They had a high proportion of experienced NCOs and officers and had been on the Somme, for the most part, for an uninterrupted period since the end of 1914. They could produce about 6,500 rifles.

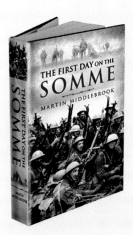
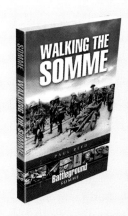

Shadows of the Great War

One Man's Battles – through Trench, Desert & Prairie

**Captain Hugh Calverley MC* 1894-1971
1/5th, and 1st Essex Regt, 1914-1918**

Archive, poems and art of an officer who fought in Gallipoli, Palestine and France.

On return to Canada he suffered mental breakdown from his war service, relieved by poetry, painting and family.

This Special Exhibition mixes the military, social and artistic, to convey the spirit of a man marked by war.

ESSEX REGIMENT MUSEUM
Oaklands Park
Moulsham St
Chelmsford
Essex
CM2 9AQ
01245 605700

12 AUGUST - 8 OCTOBER
Monday to Saturday 1000-1700
Sunday 1400-1700

Free Admission
pompadour@chelmsford.gov.uk

33

RAISING, EQUIPPING AND TRAINING THE PALS

The peace time recruiting office was not designed to process thousands of men a day. During one day in August the system processed as many men as it would have done in an entire year. In recognition of the problem the Government established offices, not only in the principal centres of all the large towns in England, but in the suburbs and in the villages and small market towns.

By Roni Wilkinson

This article was extracted from Roni Wilkinson's forthcoming book, *Pals on the Somme*, published by Pen and Sword Books Ltd., July 2006.

The numbers of men clamouring for enlistment in the forces were so great that it became near impossible to cope. Medical examinations had to be carried out, swearing in, organizing and billeting. As for providing khaki uniforms and webbing, and arming them with rifles, that seemed a long way down the line. Improvisation was the order of the day.

Incredibly, Britain was aiming at an army numbering one million then, within days of the announcement from Parliament that the British Army was to be so enlarged, there appeared on every public form of transport in London, followed by the rest of the country, posters appealing for even more volunteers. That appeal hit the eye at every turn, so that it became impossible to avoid it: 'Your King and Country Need You', with the words, 'so what are you going to do about it?' left unsaid.

The result of wholescale enlistment was that businesses

were suddenly denuded of managers, clerks, skilled workers and other key employees. It has to be said that the women of the nation made it all possible by their whole hearted support and belligerent urging of the young men:

They should be compelled to take up arms in our defence. It is far better and easier to grieve over an honest loss one than it is to find our breath quicken, our teeth clench, and our face blush with shame for anyone dear to us. If it comes to the point that all men are forced to go to war and scarce any are left, as in plucky Belgium, then I am willing to drill and fight than harm shall come to older women or children than myself. My own children I would willingly leave in God's care.

Those passionate words, which appeared in the press, of a young housewife named Rose Green Barry, served as a

Townsmen of all social backgrounds who answered Kitchener's call to arms. Here the 1st Barnsley Pals Battalion en masse at their local camp.

typical example of feminine support being generated in 1914. The nationalistic fervour was not an isolated case as women throughout Europe sent their men to war without flinching.

THE PALS PHENOMENON

In the Liverpool newspapers on 27th August 1914, there appeared an article by the Rt. Hon. The Earl of Derby in which he suggested that businessmen who were interested in serving their country might wish to join a battalion of comrades. A meeting was advertised for the following evening to be held at the Territorial drill hall of the 5th Battalion The King's (Liverpool Regiment). He personally wrote to the proprietors of the large businesses in and around Liverpool explaining the national situation and suggesting that they encourage those among their work force, so inclined, to enlist immediately.

He, like so many others, believed, that the war with Germany would be over in a matter of months and that the men would be able to return to their previous employment after a brief military sabbatical.

In *Liverpool Pals* Graham Maddocks describes for us that historic meeting which took place on a warm August Sunday evening:

> *Long before 7.30, on the evening of August 28th, St Annes's Street was crowded with eager young men trying to get into the drill hall. Those inside found that the hall was packed to capacity, and men were standing in the aisles, the doorways and even the stairs. When Lord Derby arrived and stepped onto the platform to address the multitude, his welcome was tumultuous, and this was only matched by the cheering and throwing of hats in the air which accompanied the news that Derby's brother Ferdinand was to command the new battalion when it was formed. It was obvious to Lord Derby even then, that there were more than enough men present to form one battalion.*

In his speech Lord Derby said that he would be sending Lord Kitchener that very night a telegram to say that, not one but two battalions had been formed.

> *We have got to see this through to the bitter end and dictate our terms of peace in Berlin, if it takes every man and every penny in this country.*

It was during that stirring speech that he referred to 'Pals', battalions comprising around 1,000 men, where friends from the same office would fight shoulder to shoulder. The example had indeed been set and the idea of Pals took off swelling further the Kitchener New Army ranks.

The following morning massive queues of men formed up outside St George's Hall. In acknowledgement and anticipation of the whole Pals' concept, and in response to Lord Derby's direct appeal to businesses and organizations, separate tables had been placed for each of the main areas of commerce in the city. Thus, for example, office employees of the shipping lines, Cunard and White Star could be sure of staying together as the battalions were formed. There were tables for men working at the Corn Trade Association, General Brokers, Cotton Association, The Seed Oil and Cake Trade Association, Fruit and Wool Brokers, The Law Society and Chartered Accountants and Bank and Insurance Offices. The Stock Exchange employees actually formed up in ranks of four and were marched to be attested.

Once inside St George's Hall each man gave his personal details to one of the clerks at the tables. Then small groups of men moved to another table where magistrates swore them in, each man holding up a copy of the Bible. From there they lined up outside nearby rooms

'We have got to see this through to the bitter end and dictate our terms of peace in Berlin, if it takes every man and every penny in this country.'

where medical examinations were carried out.

All the activity was overseen by Lord Derby himself and he noted the numbers of men who had been recruited and, with the medical examinations taking up the time, when the number reached 1,050 men he halted the proceedings. He had his first battalion made up of groups of friends, chums or pals. Those waiting outside were told to return in two days' time. By the following Monday, in just over a week, over 3,000 men had been recruited, sufficient for three battalions. It was remarkable in that men had already been taken into other Service battalions, Royal Navy and Mercantile Marine. A fourth Liverpool Pals' battalion was formed within eight weeks with sufficient men for two reserve battalions. The six battalions were in the King's (Liverpool Regiment) and were numbered 17th, 18th, 19th, 20th, 21st and 22nd.

MIDDLE-CLASS AND PROFESSIONAL CLASS VOLUNTEERS

News of the recruiting success at Liverpool was reported in the national and regional newspapers. That in turn prompted 'letters to the editor' and editorial features clamouring for similar formations to be raised in their own city or town.

Birmingham's non-manual workers in the city's commercial district were a-buzz with the possibility that a special battalion, just for them, might be raised. The Deputy Lord Mayor, prompted by the public response to the idea, sought advice from Birmingham's most senior Territorial officers as to how it could best be achieved. Later, in a press interview, he explained that the middle class men, obviously of officer material, were too numerous for the relatively limited number of commissions available in the Army. It was his considered opinion that this fact was causing them to hold back from joining the colours. However, he went on to explain that should a battalion be formed where men could serve together as private soldiers in companies, among those of their own class, then there would be an immediate response.

One of the senior Territorial officers, Lieutenant-Colonel Ludlow, agreed with the Deputy Lord Mayor that:

> the class from which the men should be drawn would include school teachers, clerks, articled pupils, shop assistants, warehousemen, farmers, corporation officials and others.

He added that each profession and trade would find its own special quota, and that Birmingham University and Old Boys could also serve together in the same company within such a special battalion.

It had become noticeable that the middle class men were not coming forward and one stinging letter was published in the *Birmingham Daily Mail* that summed the situation up:

> To anyone who has seen the recruiting parades through the city during the last few days the question, 'do we deserve to win?' surely has occurred. The recruits with one or two excep-

A mix of newly enlisted labourers and office workers.

tions, have been composed entirely of the so-called working classes, while the streets have been lined with young fellows wearing good clothes, looking superciliously on. Will these 'knuts' never realize that for the men whom they refuse to mix with, they would have to learn to shout 'Hoch! Hoch!' and the flappers and the barmaids, whom their life's work seems to be to fascinating, will be treated as the Belgian women have been treated by the Germans.

There would have been a natural reluctance by some to mix with men of a different and lower social class – it was all a matter of upbringing and status.

Following the phenomenal success at Liverpool two students at Sheffield University approached the University Vice-Chancellor, Mr H.A.L. Fisher, with a suggestion for a Sheffield University battalion. Fisher readily supported the idea and at the conclusion of one of his war lectures held at the Victoria Hall, Sheffield on 1st September 1914, he announced that a special committee had secured permission from the War Office to raise a Service Battalion which would be numbered to the York and Lancaster Regiment. It would be called 'The Sheffield University and City Special Battalion' (later to become simply the 'City Battalion'). Volunteers were sought from the professional classes, especially those from the university, ex-public school men, lawyers, clerks and journalists. Among them were those men who had tried to obtain commissions, but had not been successful. An advert in the *Sheffield Daily Telegraph* for recruits to the 'Sheffield University and City Special Battalion' announced to would-be volunteers: 'Intended primarily for Professional and Business Men and their Office Staffs.' It stopped short of carrying the words 'others need not apply'. In the event there were some notable exceptions when, somehow or other, some railway workers and miners, mainly from the nearby town of Penistone, ended up being accepted.

The City of Leeds, likewise, was roused to form a Pals battalion from its middle class.

The *Yorkshire Evening Post*, in an editorial of the same day, reported on the raising of the Liverpool Pals and suggested a similar 'Friends Battalion' for Leeds, 'perhaps composed of the vast, and as yet, untapped recruiting ground of the middle class population engaged in commercial pursuits'. The matter was already in hand. Lieutenant Colonel J. Walter Stead, a Leeds solicitor and former commanding officer of the 7th Battalion (Leeds Rifles), The Prince of Wales's Own (West Yorkshire Regiment), TF, had already set the raising of a Pals battalion in motion. A recruiting poster invited, 'Business men show your patriotism' and they were reminded that 'your country needs you her peril is great'. Banners appeared spanning the streets and appealing to the middle-classes with the words 'Businessmen of Leeds. Your King and Country Need You. Join the Leeds City Battalion.'

The committee of prominent dignatries formed to administer the raising of the 'Leeds City Battalion' included leading clergymen, the Vicar of Leeds, Dr Bickersteth; Bishop of Leeds, Dr Cowgill and President of the Leeds Free Church Council, Revd. John Anderson.

In Manchester the appeal to the middle class was also unashamedly direct. At a meeting of the Manchester Home Trade Association held on Monday 24th August 1914 it was agreed that recruiting should be directed towards the clerks and warehousemen employed in the numerous commercial businesses in the city. The new War Service battalion would be known as the Manchester Clerks' and Warehousemen's Battalion. An organizing committee was formed and a fund set up to finance the provision of uniforms and equipment. The dignatries and businessmen present pledged a sum of £15,000. A telegram was immediately sent to the War Office offering to raise and finance a battalion of local men at the expense of the city.

Within three days the Manchester battalion received official blessing:

> Your telegram just received. Hope you will be able to raise a battalion in Manchester and thus give your signal help to the armed forces of the Crown. Any man joining the battalion will be doing a patriotic deed, and I shall hope to welcome them in the army, where their comrades await them. Will give you every assistance. Let me know how you succeed.
>
> Kitchener.

As soon as the news became public through the pages of the *Manchester Guardian* men flocked to the designated recruiting office at the Artillery HQ in the city. In order to identify genuine clerks and warehouse men, and so ensure their being given first place, enlistment tickets were issued through the relevant firms. The response was so overwhelming that the personnel at the Drill Hall, including the two doctors carrying out the medical examinations, were unable to cope.

The forming of Pals' battalions was deemed to be the answer to a problem that was being recognized everywhere. Nationally, recruiting was going well but in Hull, as in Leeds, Sheffield, Birmingham and other cities, it was not as good as the authorities had hoped. Letters to the local papers suggested solutions. One correspondent, who went under the pseudonym 'Middle Class', wrote to the *Hull Daily Mail* that many men were not joining the colours because they did not like the idea of having to herd with all types of men now being enlisted,

Lord Lieutenant of the East Riding of Yorkshire, Lord Nunburnholme, met with Lord Kitchener and it was agreed that Hull would raise a battalion for the East Yorkshire Regiment called the 'Commercial Battalion' or officially, the 7th (Hull) Battalion. In the first day of recruiting for the 'Commercial Battalion' 695 men were attested. Within a week the battalion was at full complement. The idea was working and a further battalion was got under way designated 'Tradesmen' and in three days had reached full strength. Following the Second Hull Battalion came the 'Sportsmen Battalion' and by October it too had reached over 1,000. And still they came. Lord Kitchener gave permission to raise a fourth. The Fourth Hull Battalion was known as "T'Others' because it took any fit man regardless of their class or trade.

Because of the way in which the Hull battalions had been recruited there was bound to be incidents – or accusations – of snobbery. One private soldier in the 'Tradesmen Battalion' commented at the time that the men in the Second, Third, and Fourth battalions felt that the First battalion 'Commercials' considered themselves a cut above the others. It was referred to as a 'nobs' battalion. 'The Commercials used to snob you a bit, they was all clerks and teachers.'

LOWER WORKING CLASS

In the mining town of Barnsley, news of the raising of Pals' battalions in Liverpool prompted civic leaders to attempt something similar. The usual procedure was followed: a telegram to Lord Kitchener offering to raise a battalion of 1,000 plus men. The formal reply from the War Office served as the impetus to 'get the ball rolling'. In Barnsley's case they did not wait for official blessing but surged ahead without waiting for a reply. The first public meeting took place at the Staincross Picture Palace, 1st September 1914.

In another pit village in the Barnsley coalfield, Little Houghton, men completing the day shift flocked to the recreation ground to hear their local branch representative of the Yorkshire Miners' Association address them.

After singing the National Anthem the men surged to the colliery offices and upwards of 200 handed in their names. The following morning they were taken by motor coaches to the outskirts of Barnsley. There, they were formed up into four ranks and marched, as best they could, to the Public Hall in town to join other volunteers already gathered there. Along the way they sang with great gusto *It's a Long Way to Tipperary*. They were of course in their best civilian suits – mostly navy blue serge – and just about every man wore the popular style head gear of the day, a large floppy flat cap, consequently uniformity of a type was achieved.

Meanwhile, over the Pennines, desperate circumstances added impetus to the recruiting drive. In the summer of 1914 East Lancashire suffered a recession in the cotton industry. In the town of Accrington one of the largest employers, Howard and Bulloughs, were still closed after a dispute which had lasted ten weeks. Even the war with its insatiable demand for raw materials had not brought about a settlement. This company alone had employed 4,500 men and their families. They were having to exist on lockout pay of £1 a week, or in some instances, ten shillings. In total more than 7,000 cotton workers were unemployed or working part time in the town of Accrington. Six hundred families were on relief and each day 700 children received a hot meal at Accrington Town Hall under the 1906 Necessitous Children's (Provision of Meals) Act.

In that situation poverty was added to that of patriotism providing a powerful incentive to join the colours. For a man to be a soldier in the company of his friends and to be paid £1. 1s. a week (this included billeting allowance) to stay at home with his family, proved irresistible. Everyone was saying that the war would be over by Christmas and joining the Accrington battalion was for just as long as the war lasted. It all seemed too good to miss – a temporary respite from poverty with a paid adventure thrown in.

Two brigades of Pals were raised from among the large population crowded around the Rivers Tyne and Wear. Coal mines, iron and steel works, ship building yards meant that there was a large immigrant community originating from Scotland and Ireland.

The Tyneside Irish took longer to get under way, but was however, fortunate in having a number of ex-regular soldiers join at the start. They were men who had served with the Connaught Rangers and the Royal Irish, and had seen action in the Sudan and against the Boers in South Africa. Their experience was invaluable in the training of raw recruits.

In absence of uniforms, initially, the men were supplied with coloured arm bands: the Tyneside Irish wore green and the Tyneside Scottish a tartan one. The Newcastle Commercials wore a red lanyard.

Recruiting to the Tyneside Irish carried on apace and by December it was looking like a third battalion would be viable. After Christmas members of the raising committee travelled to London to seek permission for a fourth battalion. Like Manchester (two City brigades), Salford, Hull and the Tyneside Scottish, Tyneside Irish would produce an entire brigade consisting of four battalions for Lord Kitchener.

BILLETS, EQUIPPING AND TRAINING

Throughout the north, army camps were being constructed to accommodate Kitchener's battalions. Usually land was either Corporation owned or donated by landowners and situated in moorland areas. Within a matter of weeks roads, water and gas were laid on.

The West Yorkshire Regiment, the City of Leeds Battalion, had a ready-made camp (almost) at Colsterdale where huts recently used to house navvies employed on reservoir construction provided a base. Consequently, the battalion was in proper hutted accommodation by the end of September, months ahead of other Kitchener's Pals' Battalions. D Company was allotted the huts and the other Companies went under canvas until the camp could be completed.

At Liverpool, where the Pals' concept originated, the four battalions were spread around the district, training at various locations, sports grounds and parks, the men returning to their homes each day. Apart from the First Pals which was billetted in an old watch factory. Lord Derby decided to use his property at Knowsley Park to house the brigade and plans were drawn up. By the end of January all four battalions of the King's (Liverpool Regiment) were in hutted camp together.

To the west of Sheffield, in the foothills of the Pennines, an area was chosen as the location for the camp to house the City Battalion, 12th Service Battalion York and Lancaster Regiment. The surrounding moors, it was reasoned, would prove to be a handy training ground for a British infantry battalion. The land at the head of Rivelin valley had been used pre-war by the Territorial Army as an artillery range. In the 1939-1945 conflict, a prisoner of war camp would be set up in the vicinity and contain some hard-core Nazis as inmates. Council contractors constructed the City Battalion camp at Redmires and before it was fully completed the battalion marched out in pouring rain to take up residence on Saturday 5th December 1914. They had recently received delivery of 600 obselete rifles, enough to make a reasonable impression on the crowds who gathered along the route. Meanwhile, the neighbouring Pals' Battalion, the First Barnsleys, had still to make do with broom handles for arms drill.

A pleasant, wooded slope on the outskirts of the village of Silkstone had been acquired as the site for the 13th Service Battalion York and Lancaster Regiment. At 11 o'clock, Sunday morning 20th December, the First Barnsley Pals marched from their temporary billets at the Public Hall in town to Newhall Camp, Silkstone.

BRIGADES AND DIVISIONS

In some instances, where men were billeted over a wide area, training had been difficult at battalion strength. One estimate suggests over 800,000 men were housed in hired buildings, church halls, private homes, (War Office regulations stipulated that men should not be billeted on licensed premises). Because of the diaspersion, larger formation training would have proved nigh impossible. Consequently, hutted camps were thrown up throughout the British Isles, each one capable of housing an entire British Army division, 18,000 men. Battalions that had not trained together with fellow battalions in the same brigade were inspected by a brigade general and passed as ready for the next phase of training.

In the case of 94 Brigade a newly constructed camp on Cannock Chase in Staffordshire would be the meeting up camp for two battalions of Barnsley Pals, the Sheffield City battalion and Accrington Pals. Inevitably, men were moving into hutments that were half built. It was the month of May 1915, when soldiers began arriving at Rugeley railway station. It was a four and a half mile march to the hutments on Cannock Chase.

The time arrived at the end of May 1915 when the

battalions of 94 Brigade were officially handed over to the War Office. From that day on, the local authorities of Accrington, Sheffield and Barnsley were free from the responsibilities associated with those four battalions.

Because of the hot summer of 1915 the heathland was constantly catching fire and the soldiers were often engaged in firefighting. Also the chase was alive with wildlife and that gave some of the men the opportunity to employ a former skill, that of poacher. According to those interviewed for the Pals' series, gambling was rife among the men. Not only playing cards but a game known as 'Crown and Anchor' was endemic throughout the British Army. Attempts to stop the game proved futile. When General Douglas Haig took overall command of the British Expeditionary Force in December 1915 he made it a penal offence to be caught playing 'Crown and Anchor'. He ruled that after three convictions a man would face a court martial.

At the end of July 1915 the order came for the battalions of 94th Brigade to move to the Fourth Army Training Centre at Ripon in North Yorkshire. The whole area around Ripon was congested with troops of Kitchener's Army.

Three Brigades were brought together to make up the 31st Division. It truly was a Pals' division:

92nd Brigade consisted of four battalions of the East Yorkshire Regiment and were 10th (Hull, Commercials), 11th (Hull, Tradesmen), 12th (Hull, Sportsmen), 13th (Hull, T'others).

93rd Brigade consisted of three battalions of the West Yorkshire Regiment, (Leeds Pals), 16th (First Bradford), 18th (Second Bradford), and one battalion of the Durham Light Infantry, (18th Durham Pals).

94th Brigade consisted of one battalion of the East Lancashire Regiment (11th Accrington Pals) and three battalions of the York and Lancaster Regiment 12th (Sheffield City), 13th (First Barnsley Pals), 14th (Second Barnsley Pals).

The Divisional Pioneer battalion was the 12th King's Own Yorkshire Light Infantry.

A series of inspections by various generals followed culminating in the new commander of the division, Major General Wanless O'Gowan, who would remain with the division to the end of the war. Battalion commanders, on the other hand, would be replaced by younger men as active service loomed closer with the move of the 31st Division to Salisbury Plain.

The training received on Salisbury Plain was more in keeping with the realities of trench fighting taking place across the Channel. The Lewis gun was supplied to the battalions and gun teams, each consisting of six men, were formed to operate them. The men were introduced to the Mills bomb, a hand grenade with a four-second fuse. This weapon was proving invaluable in the trench fighting on the Western Front. Another feature of twentieth century fighting was barbed wire; experience in the handling and construction of barbed wire defences was given.

By the month of November 1915 rumour of a move abroad began to circulate throughout 31st Division, and the issue of pith helmets served to reinforce the rumour. Author David Bilton in his work on the *Hull Pals* highlights the last minute changing decisions of the High Command. Quoting a private in the 10th Battalion, Hull Commercials, he says that the soldier, later to become an officer, wrote in his diary:

December 4th: equipment for France issued.

December 6th: equipment for France withdrawn. Pith helmets and puggarees were handed out and it was rumoured that camel humps would be issued. Everyone was certain that the battalion was going to India, or Mesopotamia, or Arabia, or Egypt or somewhere else.

The official history of the 11th Battalion, Hull Tradesmen, records a similiar story when it reports that gas helmets were issued in preparation for service in France only for them to be suddenly withdrawn and replaced by 1,025 sun helmets. It would seem that many men in the division recalled marching to the trains that would take them to the departure ports in pouring rain – wearing their recently issued pith helmets.

Throughout the month of December the battalions of 31st Division were on their way to Egypt to defend the Suez Canal from the Turks.

Other Pals' divisions were already facing the enemy having crossed to France in October and November. The 34th Division, which consisted of four battalions of Tyneside Irish, four battalions of Tyneside Scottish, two battalions of Edinburgh City, the Cambridge Battalion and the Grimsby Chums, sailed for France in January 1916. However the first across the Channel were the Manchester and Liverpool Pals.

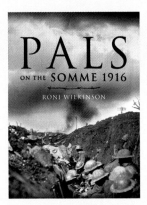

'As soon as we got
into No Mans
Land the Germans
opened fire with
their heavy
machine-guns.
We dropped like
nine-pins.'

SERGEANT BILL DUTTON - 1ST PALS.

EXPERIENCES OF THE SALFORD PALS – THE 1ST & 2ND PALS' ATTACK

On the night of 30th June 1st Pals moved up from Bouzincourt. Every few yards the platoons were momentarily lit by the flash of explosions. Even shouted orders proved impossible to hear. Nevertheless, the men moved into the familiarity of their line under the cover of darkness and the crashing sounds of shellfire, being in position by 1.00 a.m.

By Michael Stedman

This article was extracted from Michael Stedman's book, *The Somme 1916 & Other Experiences of the Salford Pals* and is reproduced here by permission of Pen and Sword Books Ltd.

THE 1ST AND 2ND PALS' ATTACK

The trenches which they took over from the 'Skins' had been badly shattered by the persistence of the German shelling and provided only minimal shelter. Simultaneously the 2nd Pals moved out of Black Horse dugouts into support in the French Street evacuation trenches and around Johnstone Post, roughly 300 yards behind the two assault battalions; the 1st Pals and the 16th Northumberland Fusiliers. As this move got underway:

...there was a ruined village [Authuille] to traverse, where shells had set fire to one of the ruined houses, and the red glare added to a further awesomeness to the scene. Leaving the village we proceeded along the communication trench, and the shells began to fall about us in greater number, but we kept steadily on. At last we entered the communication trench leading to the assembly trench. This lay though a thick wood [Thiepval], and enemy shellfire had brought down heavy trees, which particularly blocked the way and made progress slow. We were almost at our rendezvous when a crash in front warned those behind that things were not well. The party halted and the order was passed down: 'Officer wanted at the front at once.' An officer started off crushing past the crouching men, and then whiz crash, a whiz bang fired enfilade along the trench fell amongst us, followed by others.

This relief cost the 2nd Pals four killed, including Sergeant W. Taylor and T. H. [Harry] Potter (15166), together with seven wounded, including Lieutenant Waugh of D company and 2nd Lieutenant Powell which

necessitated Captain Tweed taking command of both support companies behind the 1st Pals.

Throughout that cloudless night a thick ground mist rolled through the trenches and valleys. Very few of the men could sleep through the erratic din and glare of shelling and the damp cold of their contemplation.

One man who had been anguished that night was Bill Dutton. Earlier in June his great friend from Salford, Peter Fensome, had been shot in the leg. By contrast with some of the more dreadful sights which he had seen this was a relatively minor wound and Bill had been pleased to think that his mate would miss today's events. Since their days in Conway the boys had been great friends, although once arguing so fiercely that their mothers had to issue instructions to patch things up! Now, in the blackness of the night of 30th June, they unexpectedly met again.

I saw Peter coming along and we put our arms around each other. I said, 'What made you come

The dawn bombardment before the 'Big Push'.

back Peter?' He said they were clearing the hospitals for the coming battle and if you weren't too badly wounded, well, you volunteered to come back. He said he wanted to go over the top with the company.

SERGEANT BILL DUTTON. 1ST PALS.

As daylight began to break, the sky above Thiepval was uncluttered by clouds and ominously blue. In the sodden Ancre valley and the shattered woodlands out of which Salford's Pals would attack, the air was damp, misty and still.

In front of Thiepval the Germans clearly expected a dawn attack and their defensive barrage was initially heavy, lasting for an hour after first light at 3.30 a.m. As the sun then began its climb above the Thiepval ridge a deceptive lull in the cacophany of noise existed, shattered at 6.25 a.m., when the British bombardment intensified into a another pulverizing series of explosions which seemed to make the very air bounce and resonate. Under their feet the men could feel the vibrations and shock waves. Simultaneously gas was released from cylinders placed in No Man's Land. It drifted slowly over the rubble in front.

If nothing else it proved the continued presence of men opposite as the clanging of gas alarm bells was heard during momentary gaps amidst the blasts of explosion. Between Maison Grise and Hammerhead the Pals' officers were visibly tense and anxious. Far too much of the wire was still clearly visible in front of Thiepval, although at 6.37 a.m. the 97th Brigade to the right telephoned Divisional HQ with word that,

> 'Barely fifty yards had been covered when he was hit by a bullet, which grazed his head, whilst I got one in the arm.'

...the enemy wire on their front [west of Leipzig] completely cleared and all are satisfied there will be no hitch.

With just ten minutes to go, as the final bombardment thundered into Thiepval, A and C Companies of the 1st Pals, under command of Captain Alfred Lee Wood and Lieutenant H.C. Wright, crept forward to within 100 yards of the village, beyond the trees east of Hammerhead sap, either side of Oblong Wood and down past Thiepval Point South. In support, in Thiepval Wood, were B and D Companies, commanded by the recently promoted Captain Geoffrey Heald and Captain Ernest MacLaren. The violence being wrought by the shellfire on Thiepval in front of them convinced some that no one could possibly continue to live in that inferno. But shockingly, and contrary to all the men's expectations of this point in time, German machine guns were already being heard, firing over the thunderous sound of shells falling on Thiepval.

There would be no respite from their deadly attention.

At 7.30, the first waves from A and C Companies stood up and began to walk forward. As soon as they breasted the rise in front of Thiepval and showed themselves, scores were cut down by the inevitable, scything, machine-gun fire. Within minutes a heavy barrage began to fall on the British front line and casualties began to occur among the runners trying to maintain communication between Lieutenant Colonel Lloyd's Battalion headquarters in Bromielaw Street and the attacking companies. All the meticulous planning was nought.

Private Hutton (10204) provided one of the few eyewitness account from the midst of this disastrous scenes. Speaking of Captain Alfred Lee Wood, from Lake Hospital in Ashton-under-Lyne, he said that.

Barely fifty yards had been covered when he was hit by a bullet, which grazed his head, whilst I got one in the arm. Without pausing we went on a little further, when a second bullet struck the captain on the head, causing a nasty gash, and almost at the same moment I was shot through the leg. Turning to me Captain Lee Wood asked, 'Are you badly hit?' and I replied, 'Yes Sir, I can't go on this time.' He then ordered me to try and get back to our trench, and although I begged him to come back with me, since he was badly wounded, he said, 'No, I will get that machine gunner.

On their left the 36th (Ulster) Division's attack was going well, the 9th and 10th Royal Inniskilling Fusiliers crossing No

German machine-gun team in action. Along with accurate artillery fire they proved most effective in stopping the attacking British infantry on the Somme.

Landscape at Thiepval during Somme Battle.

Man's Land and sweeping across the front and support trenches towards the Crucifix and Srhwaben Redoubt, This vital distraction on Thiepval's right flank gave a pitiably small number of the 1st Pals in A Company a chance to get through the wire and enter the German trenches in front and to the north of the village. Unfortunately, no attempt at mopping up the dugouts was possible and those Salford men who had crossed the first German line then made their way to the north of Thiepval, in the direction of the Ulstermen's success, south of Schwaben Redoubt.

Nevertheless, behind those first companies, the following waves of men from B and D Companies tried desperately to get up to the enemy's trenches through the counter-barrage now sweeping No Man's Land but all efforts simply resulted in the almost instant killing or wounding of the parties moving forward. At this point the 96th Brigade still believed that the advance was going smoothly although communication had become impossible.

Private George Knight (10163) then serving in the machine-gun section, from C Company, 1st Salfords, who was amongst those killed. SIMMONDS

The leading and support Companies kept their proper distance and all lines got into the enemy trenches. At 7.45AM connection between Bn. H.Q. in BROMIELAW STREET, which had been maintained by a chain of messengers, was broken owing to several casualties due to M.G. fire both from front and flanks.

In No Man's Land those soldiers who had survived the first shattering moments were in a desperate position. Many of the men were being pinned down and picked off by very accurate machine-gun and rifle fire.

As soon as we got into No Man's Land the Germans opened fire with their heavy machine guns. We dropped like nine-pins. I was the same as everyone else. I dropped into a shell hole. One officer realized how futile the attack was and told us to stay there 'till nightfall. You were shot down if you made any movement at all. We spent the day in shell holes, talking and swearing.

SERGEANT BILL DUTTON. 1ST PALS.

One of the men with whom Bill Dutton shared that shell hole was 'Boxer' Wilson. Bleeding profusely Wilson had been lacerated by his own barbed wire as he struggled to find safety from the constant machine-gun fire.

Of the four gun Vickers section from 96th Machine Gun Company, supporting the 1st Pals, all guns bar one were knocked out trying to cross No Man's Land. The remaining gun's team by then consisted of one Pprivate who brought the gun back to the front lines. Two teams of the 96th Trench Mortar Battery moved forward to Hammerhead Sap, one officer moving forward from there in an attempt to ascertain the situation of the 1st Pals but was unfortunately killed.

In the shell-pocked and cursed acres in front of Thiepval, hundreds of khaki-clad figures lay, some breathlessly motionless, some in terrible agony, some simply still under the increasing heat of a clearing blue sky. The minutes trickled by and the sound of exploding shells dulled as the bombardment lifted and began to fall on the intermediate position beyond the near edge of Thiepval plateau. As that barrage moved uselessly into the distance the machine gunners in square 25 were set for revenge after seven days' of waiting in a terrible anticipation under the 32nd Division's enormous preparatory bombardment. Their situation was even further improved when one of the two British 9.2-in howitzers, detailed to fire on enemy machine-gun posts in the Thiepval area, suffered a premature shell burst, putting itself and its partner out of action for the duration of the day.

Within minutes of their attack going in it had become impossible for the 32nd Division's observers to see what was happening.

At 7.55 the Mesnil OP reported that it was impossible to see owing to smoke. Very little shelling but a lot of machine-gun fire.

The trench mortars remained silent. It was already thought inadvisable to redirect their bombardment onto

43

Thiepval from the air. This reconnaissance photograph reveals the strength and depth of the defences within Thiepval village.

Thiepval in view of the uncertainty surrounding who was in the vicinity of the village.

One hour after the start of their assault, and more in hope than certainty, the 1st Salford Pals' adjutant reported to 32nd Divisional Headquarters that the Battalion's men had taken the German front lines. In fact, all that Lieutenant Colonel Lloyd now commanded, apart from his adjutant, was his Lewis gun officer and some twenty to thirty men held back from the attack. However, air and artillery observers now reported seeing isolated parties of British troops in and to the north and east of the village, but not one man or officer from the 1st Pals who got there would live to tell that tale. Behind those parties of the 15th Lancashire Fusiliers' men who had broken through, the German troops quickly merged from the protection of their dugouts on the right of the Salfords' attack to re-establish themselves in their own front line.

On the 1st Pals' right, zero hour had seen the utter obliteration of the 16th Northumberlands, to the south of Maison Grise Sap. As their own barrage had lifted from the German trenches opposite, the

leading waves of Newcastle men had set off,

A and B Coys moved forward in waves and were instantly fired upon by Enemy's M.G & snipers. The Enemy stood upon their parapet & waved to our men to came on & picked them off with rifle fire. The Enemy's fire was so intense that the advance was checked & the waves, or what was left of them, were forced to lie down.

Line after line of men from each subsequent company had leaped out of their trenches only to meet with the same fate as their predecessors. It was not until 8.20 that it became known at Division that the situation here was desperate and that more barrage was required on the German front line. Behind the 16th Northumberlands their machine-gun section was brought into the front line to provide indirect supporting fire across the unfolding catastrophe in front of them.

The failure of the Tynesider's attack meant a day of unremitting horror and difficulty for the few surviving men of the 96th Brigade's assault battalions and their support, the 2nd Pals. The behaviour of the 2nd Salfords that day was both tragic

THE SALFORD PALS' OBJECTIVE

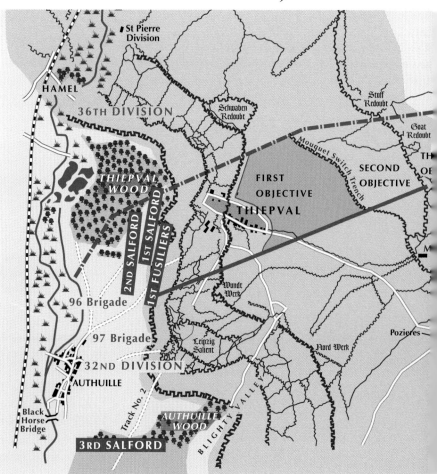

and exemplary, motivated as much by the plight of their pals as by the tactical military imperative of taking Thiepval.

A and C Companies were in support of the Northumberlands, in French Street trench behind Gemmel Trench. B and D Companies were behind their own 1st Pals. When the men from Newcastle were so savagely cut down, Lieutenant Nelson Alien brought A Company into Gemmell Trench at 7.55, just behind the Northumberland's front line trenches. At 8.10 Allen's A Company moved into the front lines, between Maison Grise and Hamilton Avenue, From where No. 1 Platoon went over the top at 8.20 under the command of 2nd Lieutenant W.E. Foss, in a vain attempt to support the failed attack made by the 16th Northumberland Fusiliers. One man who was there, Sergeant E. Wild (12167), later recounted his experiences whilst recovering in a Stockport hospital, from bullet and shrapnel wounds. Sergeant Wild was one of the men from No. l platoon of the 2nd Pals who had gone over to support the 16th Northumberland Fusiliers at 8.20. He initially took shelter against the road bank leading from Skinner Street in the direction of Thiepval. Subsequently he and four others found a shell hole more effective. All five were already struck by bullets. Further injuries were sustained as shrapnel continued to tear into the earth around the group. They were joined in the hole by a solitary German prisoner who was desperately making his way to the British lines. Like many other men that day one of this group, looking over the rim of the shell hole in search of further prisoners, was immediately shot through the head, so severe and accurate was the machine-gun and rifle fire.

Seeing this disastrous situation in front, Captain Roger Knott ordered his men in C Company to dump their RE materials whilst he sought Colonel Ritson, commanding the 16th Northumberlands in their front line. It was clear that the 16th Northumberlands were so depleted that they would be unable to effectively man their own front line. Within Captain Knott's company 2nd Lieutenant Charles Marriot was therefore ordered to take his men down into the chaotic confines of the front line trench.

I sent a message to A Coy on our left to say what I was doing, and started to lead up a communication trench between its called Hamilton Avenue – or rather what was left of if. Gerry was plastering the whole sector with H.E., and already it was less a trench than shell holes and hummocks. Our scrambles over these were speeded by the German machine-gunners above, who weren't missing much that morning. After all these years I still clearly see certain gruesome sights, burnt into the memory, as we struggled up to the front line. Hands, feet and shin bones were protruding from the raw earth stinking of

high explosive. A smallish soldier sitting in a shell hole, elbows on knees, a sandbag over his shoulders: I lifted it to see if he were alive, and he had no head. Further on, a corporal lying doubled up and bloody. Just in case anything could be done for him I bent down to raise him a little, and his head was only attached by a bit of skin. The front trench was so blown up and gouged by H.E. that only bits of it remained, and it took some time to deploy out along it.

Meanwhile I was told that a badly-wounded officer was lying in it about twenty yards along. I got to him over a great blown-in block, bullets whizzing like wasps, and found a tall young Northumberland Fusilier lieutenant, shot through both knees, one wrist and one shoulder: the moment he got up onto the parapet the impact of the bullets had flung him backwards into the trench. I tried to bandage him up a bit (his courage was so superb I think I was weeping as I did so, which wasn't really much help) and sent an urgent call for stretcher-bearers. But there was too much to see to, I had to leave him, and never knew what happened to him. We found others like him shot straight back off the parapet; one, a sergeant, drilled through the forehead, his brains spread like hair over the back of his neck. At last we were ready, and I was bracing myself for the hideous decision to go over the top when we were saved from further massacre in the nick of time by a sweating runner with a message from the C.O. to stay put. My God, what a moment! No Man's Land, covered with bodies, was a sight I can never forget: the whole of the 16/N.F. seemed to be lying out there.

> '**I tried to bandage him up a bit (his courage was so superb I think I was weeping as I did so, which wasn't really much help) and sent an urgent call for stretcher-bearers.**'

In this position the men of A and C manned the shattered Northumberlands' line, suffering casualties throughout the day from the high explosive and shrapnel being rained on these positions.

Meanwhile, on their left, B and D Coys had been brought into the front lines twenty minutes after zero when news already suggested that men of the 1st Pals were in trouble in the area of Thiepval. Since early hours officers had awaited the moment when the courage of their men would be put to the test, anxiously consulting watches and marking the progress of the Ulstermen who could be seen on their left.

Above our heads an enemy machine gun kept spitting away defiantly. Skillfully hidden behind a wood, in the ruins of a village which was to be taken by us, it had braved the bombardment and its team off to be quite fair – very brave and capable soldiers, fired with a deadliness and accuracy which was amazing. It was drawing

45

The ground over which the Salford Pals attacked on 1st July 1916.

towards the time of our going forward. Every second we expected our first troops to silence the gun. Five minutes before eight the gun was silent. Then the Captain's voice, 'Fix bayonets,' a few pregnant minutes, and a further order, '5 and 6 over the top, and good luck, boys'.

Under the command of Captain Tweed both companies needed no encouragement to get forward to do their bit. It was, however, both desperate and hopeless. The instant the Eccles men left their trenches and revealed themselves the machine guns restarted.

Some, like young Grindley, were killed getting over, and rolled back into the trench, but through the perfect storm of lead the company went on. Ignoring the rain of death that whistled about them, they kept running from shell hole to shell hole, on and on. Pals of years' association dropped, others fell riddled with bullets never to rise again. But the cry was always 'On!' Lieut. Walton was wounded and left behind; Lieut. Brooman who had charge of 5th and 6th platoons, was well ahead [at the cross roads beyond Hammerhead sap], and had already been hit twice. [Tweed] rushed up to the 7th and 8th platoon, who had lost nearly all their N.C.0.'s, and leaping out of a shell hole urged them to follow. A few seconds hesitation to face the lightning death above them, and then Private Bradshaw leaped out and called again, to be followed by all the others. Forward, ever forward. But by this time a very few men were left, and a sheltering bank in 'No Man's Land' became a haven of refuge. What was left of the company stayed there for two hours unable to move.

'Some, like young Grindley, were killed getting over, and rolled back into the trench, but through the perfect storm of lead the company went on.'

A succinct entry in the battalion War Diary recorded just how few of the Eccles Company had in fact made it to the shelter of the road embankment.

At 8 o'clock the first line of B Co-advanced but came under M.G. fire whilst crossing QUEEN'S X BANK, the other lines and D Co followed. The front line reached the cross roads beyond HAMMERHEAD SAP but had suffered severely from M.G. fire from direction of THIEPVAL, Captain TWEED reckoning that his Coy was only about 40 strong at this point.

This tiny force of men had, as yet, only covered fifty yards in the direction of Thiepval and a further hour would elapse before they would be ordered to reinforce the 1st Pals. Behind them three of the officers and many men with D Company were already casualties from the intense air bursts of shrapnel being hurled at the Queen's Cross Trench and bank area. Tweed initially had run back to tell the remaining 2nd Lieutenant, Jones, to keep his men under cover until B Company could be seen to make progress.

At 9.10 a.m., Major General Rycroft ordered the 96th Brigade to use the supports to push round the northern edge of Thiepval to meet up with the 1st Pals and the right of the 36th Division at the 'Crucifix' on the southern tip of Schwaben Redoubt. Unfortunately the 2nd Royal Inniskillings were not as yet available. Their headquarters and two companies arrived at Johnstone Post at 10.00 a.m. One further company was being held in reserve at the Bluff. Only one company of the 'Skins' was in the area of the 2nd Salfords, sheltering within French Street since 8.55. This clearly meant that what was left of B and D Companies of the 2nd Salford Pals would be responsible for the attack on their own.

The remaining small numbers of B Company tried to get forward through the trees towards the edge of the village. Immediately the intensity of machine-gun fire from the Thiepval Fort area became overwhelming. Small groups of men were pinned down outside the wire by the machine-gun fire which tracked above their heads. Some desperate men took their lives in their own hands in attempts to reach their friends. They were simply cut down as they bunched to get through the one obvious gap in the wire. Other men, under the extraordinarily brave command of 2nd Lieutenant Edward Brooman who had already been twice hit by bullets, stayed under the wire all morning in the search for a way through. Under the road embankments, around Hammerhead Sap, and in any shell hole around Oblong Wood dozens of men crouched and swore and prayed for darkness.

Captain Tweed tried to work a number of parties forward himself after having reconnoitred possible routes through the trees. Corporal Sharpies (11757) and Privates Howell (10266) and Jones tried and were almost immediately cut down. As soon as Private Fiddes (12491), Tweed's orderly, left the safety of the embankment to obtain instructions from Battalion Headquarters he was instantly shot, but was pulled back into shelter. While writing his next message Tweed's notebook was hit by a bullet and flung from his grasp. Brooman was hit for a third time.

Taking enormous risk Tweed dragged Brooman back to the comparative safety of his front line trenches in search of orders to pull the men out. By 10.30 a.m., orders were received from Major General Rycroft requesting the men to hold fast while attempts were made to capitalize on success by the 36th Division and turn the Thiepval defences from the north. The Ulstermen had made incredible inroads into the German defences north of Thiepval even though their right flank was being eroded by the persistent and deadly storm of machine guns firing in enfilade from Thiepval village. By 9.30 the 36th Division was believed to be moving on point Cl2 (R13d6/9), north of Schwaben Redoubt and north-east of St. Pierre Division. An hour later the German prisoners from the Schwaben Redoubt area were running into 36th Division's lines 'with hands up in considerable numbers'. By 10.45 the two machine guns firing from close by Thiepval Château were still causing heavy casualties amongst the Ulstermen's 107th Brigade. Nevertheless, by 11,00 a.m., men from that Brigade were up at the Mouquet Farm – Grandcourt lines and the German situation in Thiepval was becoming critical.

Unfortunately the artillery reports reaching 32nd Divisional Headquarters were geographically rather vague, although positive about the presence of Salford men in Thiepval at R25cd.

At 10.55 am the artillery report that 16th N.F are over the front line and 15th Lancs Fusrs are somewhere in THIEPVAL. There is no informa-tion from Northumberland Fusiliers.

By 11.40 Major General Rycroft at last managed to contact Lieutenant General Morland in his observation tree at Engelbelmer. Between them a plan was devised to extend the attacks on Thiepval by a further artillery bombardment, including heavy howitzers, of the reverse

Brigadier General Yatman, whose belief in the presence of the Salford Pals in Thiepval had a profound effect on the battle for control of this area throughout 1st July.
HISTORICAL RECORDS OF THE 16TH NFS P.19

of the spur, the Wundt-werk, the Nordwerk and the trenches at the head of Blighty Valley. By noon X Corps had arranged the bombardment of these positions from 12.16 until 1.30 p.m. Rightly or wrongly the shelling of Thiepval itself was again postponed in view of Brigadier General Yatman's continued belief, at 11.45, in the presence of the 1st Pals there. Morland was told by Rycroft that Brigadier-General Yatman had already arranged to send companies of the 96th Brigade's reserve battalion, the 2nd Royal Inniskilling Fusiliers, to prepare to penetrate north of the village, with orders then to turn south, taking the position of Thiepval in reverse and cutting off the route of any reinforcements moving along Zollern Graben (Lancashire Lane) from the direction of Goat Redoubt and Courcelette.

The reluctance of Thiepval to fall was having a disastrous impact on the 36th Division's chances of holding on to the gains at Schwaben Redoubt. At 11.50 the 109th Brigade headquarters reported that machine-gun fire from Thiepval was preventing all movement across the German front and support lines, making it impossible for them to get any fresh troops, ammunition or water forward to the men who were clinging on in the redoubt. Along the Thiepval Road above Hammerhead Sap piles of bodies, Ulstermen, Inniskillings and Lancashire Fusiliers were literally heaped in lines where the machine guns in

2nd Lieutenant Laurence Price. Eighteen years of age and only with the 2nd Pals since 1st June. Having been posted from the 4th Lancashire Fusiliers, he survived the events of 1st July. WHIPPY

Thiepval had cut them down throughout the day.

Those men from the 2nd Salford Pals who were still left alive, and able to crawl back, had been withdrawn into Queen's Cross Street trench, to regroup and prepare to attack again with the Inniskillings. At 1.30 two companies of the 2nd 'Skins' together with the parties of the 2nd Salford Pals attacked towards the north-west comer of Thiepval in a desperate attempt to close the gap on the 36th Division's right flank. They met with exactly the same fate as the Pals had earlier in the day. A further attack, by men of 1/6th and part of the 1/8th West Yorks, mounted during the afternoon at 4.00 p.m., also met with disaster. At best, these attacks by the 146th Brigade of the 49th Division could be said to have lacked co-ordination. The other two Brigades were ordered to circulate aimlessly behind the Thiepval Wood area throughout the day. Anything that moved in front of the wood became an easy prey to the enemy machine gunners in Thiepval. Writing later to the family of Private Fiddes, Captain Tweed said that the orderly had been bandaged. However,

> When the surviving members of the Company retired he appeared to have been hit again, and was unconscious. A number of wounded were lying in the open, and the enemy later in the afternoon riddled them with bullets. Another attack was made by fresh troops with no better success, and some hundreds of bodies lay in the open...

West of the Ancre, watching from the 32nd Division's Advanced Report Centre on the Bouzincourt Road, 2nd Lieutenant (later Captain) Edgar Lord of the 15th LFs pondered the circumstances which had forced him to miss these events. As an officer attached to the Battalion since mid May, Lord had had little experience with the unit, having been injured by an explosion at the trench mortar demonstration a month earlier, in which Major Robert Thomas, the second in command, was killed.

> A boiling hot day. without a breath of wind and down the dusty road came men with wounds of every description. A few of the worst cases came on the ambulances, which were in very small supply, but carts, wagons, lorries, limbers, water tanks and any vehicles which would give a lift were crammed to the utmost. The walking cases were choked with dust, staggering along between the timbers, sometimes helping each other forming human crutches, most of them wearing blood stained bandages, and many in improvised splints. The agony on their weary faces told a weary tale of experiences well-nigh beyond recounting, as all had only just escaped the longest Journey of all.
>
> I helped as I could by buying chocolates, biscuits and giving draughts of water from my bottle, but all along the road men laid down for the last time, being wounded worse than they knew.

North of Thiepval the men of the Ulster Division were gradually weakened throughout the day's fighting.

During the morning patrols had been driven away from the village by grenades and the intensity of fire, but other patrols towards Mouquet Farm along the switch trench had shown that it might well have been possible to take Thiepval in reverse since this area was not occupied by the enemy. However, it was proving impossible to sustain the 36th Division's advanced supplies of ammunition and water because of the curtain of machine-gun fire which swept Mill Road and the slopes in front of Thiepval Wood. During the afternoon two infantry counter-attacks from the directions of Grandcourt and Goat Redoubt, combined with a prolonged bombardment of the Schwaben Redoubt, exhausted the dwindling band of men. The elements of the 49th Division now detailed to support the Ulstermen came up too late to effect a change in the tactical balance of power here. By 10.00 p.m. the Ulstermen retired from the Schwaben Redoubt positions to the old German front line positions.

When the 2nd Pals from B and D Coys were brought

The British trenches filled with wounded within minutes of the offensive getting under way.

An advanced dressing station taking in walking wounded on the Somme.

together for rollcall in their trench below Thiepval that night, only Tweed and seventeen others remained uninjured. By contrast, A and C Companies were still comparatively intact. As the 2nd Inniskillings moved into the trenches to relieve the Salfords that night at 11 p.m., C Company of the 2nd Pals was moved right to hold the front line between Greenock Street (R31a1/5) and Skinner Street (R31a2/2).

The 1st Pals were decimated, having only three officers and 150 men left in the entire battalion. That night these remaining men were withdrawn to the bluff at Authuille. Writing in his own Battalion's diary within hours of these events, the 2nd Pals' Lieutenant Colonel Abercrombie already knew the cause of the catastrophe.

It is evident that the bombardment failed to dislodge the protected M.G.s in the Thiepval defences and it is probable that some of these were in advanced positions nearer to our lines than we had supposed; there must also have been some M.G.s with a high command, for men crawling were instantly detected and fired on. During our bombardment before the attack enemy M.G.s could be heard firing from several positions.

These were the machine guns which had been sited within strengthened saps, just a few yards in front of the German front lines at Thiepval. The menace of these guns was now clearly understood and accounted for, although that knowledge was too late to stem the continuing impetus behind the Somme offensive which was now destined for four further bloodied months duration.

Most of their machine guns were in steel rail and concrete nests, proof against anything less than a direct hit by a 12-in., cunningly camouflaged in No Man's Land, and superbly sited for crossfire.

Thiepval had proved to be a quite impenetrable fortress.

The attacks this day were all too clearly destined for failure in view of the village's commanding position, the strength of the defences and the rigidity of the assault's timing which ensured that the Salford men here would attack with little more hope than that of perishing bravely. This they had most certainly achieved.

Throughout the remainder of the night the men of the 2nd Pals dug in and sheltered as best they could from the continuing bombardment of 77s and 4.2s. Parts of No Man's Land were searched and as many of the wounded as could be found were carried in.

At dark a few survivors and slightly wounded came in, but the dead were everywhere. We spent the night searching for the badly wounded and bringing in all we could. One of my chaps, Corporal Chidgey, carried in seven on his own back.

The following day was spent clearing the dismembered bodies and discarded equipment from the trenches, and repairing the parapets and revetments which had been virtually destroyed by shellfire. A further heavy bombardment of Gemmel trench and the front positions opposite Thiepval again caused casualties at 5.30 p.m. that afternoon. The 2nd Pals were relieved from their trenches by the 2nd South Lancashires at 3.00 a.m. on 3rd July, marching back to Aveluy Wood and thence on to Warloy-Baillon. Their casualties during the previous two days had been 223 men and nine officers.

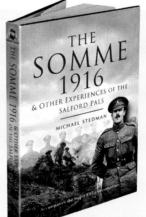

'Thiepval is both an inspiration and an education to all but it is the next generation who will need to learn most from this place.'

THE THIEPVAL VISITOR CENTRE

For almost eighty years the Memorial to the Missing has stood in brooding silence on a windswept hill overlooking the slopes which were at the epicentre of the 1916 Battle of the Somme. Without facilities, explanation or shelter the location could be both forbidding and bleak on a cold winter's day. I personally felt that the Memorial lay in danger of losing contact with the generation whose empathy was essential if the terrible costs of war were to be appreciated by today's young people.

By Michael Stedman

This article was extracted from Michael Stedman's book, *Thiepval - Battleground Series* and is reproduced here by permission of Pen and Sword Books Ltd.

That situation has now, thankfully, been changed. The development of the Thiepval Visitor Centre has ensured that this location will continue to be the focal point of remembrance and attention to the history of the Great War and the 1916 Battle of the Somme. Of course, the centre has in no way usurped the purpose of the Memorial to the Missing, but I believe that it is a magnificent addition to the powerful message which this location sends to all who visit here.

The visitor centre at Thiepval opened on 27th September 2004. Present at the opening were Emilie Poupard and Jonty Leggett, two ten-year old children, the great niece and the great nephew of two soldiers, one French and one British who were Killed in Action in the battles around Thiepval. The costs of the construction have been raised by donation and grants, perhaps the most poignant being of £102 from a 102 year old veteran of the Somme fighting, Mr Douglas Roberts. Hundreds of other individuals and commercial concerns have contributed, as well as the Department of the Somme and the European Union.

The unveiling ceremony of the Thiepval Memorial, 31st July 1932.

The building is innovative, discreet and airy. The bricks perfectly match those used by Lutyens in the nearby memorial yet the extensive use of glass and modern construction techniques ensure that the interior is beautifully illuminated and spacious. The grounds of the centre have been carefully landscaped to minimize its visual impact within the area. Incorporated into the centre is an elevated outdoor viewing area with a panoramic view across to Thiepval Wood, the Ulster Tower, the River Ancre and northwards to Serre.

The centre has been created with the express intention of providing visitors with a modern facility, providing information and explanatory materials which deal with the experience of the Great War along the Western Front, on the Somme in general and at Thiepval in particular. It has been the product of many people's commitment to the project over many years and is the foremost example of its type in France. The visitor centre lies just yards from Lutyens' Memorial to the Missing, but is discreetly placed out of site of that remarkable place. There is

The exterior of the new Visitor Centre. MICHAEL STEDMAN

ample car and coach parking as well as a shop selling maps, DVD copies of the films on show, books and guides to the locality. Refreshments, toilet and washroom facilities are also available at the centre, making good a problem which has made visiting this area difficult in the past. If you are engaged in a tour or walking visit to the Somme and the 1916 battlefields in particular, the visitor centre at Thiepval is an ideal place for a contemplative rest and some refreshment. The car park provides a suitable place from which to embark upon a number of walks which form a part of this guidebook.

Inside the centre visitors are met by a huge panel with photographs of a representative sample of the missing – some 600 in all. Details of these and other men are available on computers which can be accessed by visitors. The 600 photographs ensure a suitable tone inside the centre, which retains a dignified and purposeful atmosphere suited to the nearby memorial's intentions. Walking around the centre reveals numerous expansive panels which use photographs, maps and text to evocate the enormity of the events and the nature of

The view across the 18th Division's memorial toward Thiepval Wood, Connaught and Mill Road Cemeteries and the Ulster Tower. MICHAEL STEDMAN

The view across the village of Thiepval from the Memorial to the Missing. MICHAEL STEDMAN

The view towards the Memorial to the Missing from the Ancre valley and Caterpillar Wood across the scene of the Tyneside Commercials' attack on 1st July 1916. MICHAEL STEDMAN

The view towards the Memorial to the Missing from the direction of the Leipzig Salient. The track here formed the dividing line between 54 (on left) and 53 Brigades on 26th September. MICHAEL STEDMAN

the fighting. Specific attention is paid to the areas near to Thiepval and the events during 1916 and 1918 at Thiepval are dealt with in detail. Included within the displays is a moving plasma screen map which graphically narrates the changing tides of the war and which many visitors have come to regard as an invaluable aid to understanding. Many of the materials, maps and photographs are reproduced in a finely printed book which is also on sale at the centre.

The centre also provides an Audio Visual theatre with films which complement the graphic panels. The films deal with Reconstruction and Memory, the Somme Battles and the Thiepval locale in detail. In total the three films last for some fifty-seven minutes and can be seen sequentially or in isolation. Apart from contemporary footage taken during 1916 and 1918, the films contain explanation and expert analysis which will enhance any visit to the area of Thiepval and the Memorial to the Missing. These films are available on DVD and can be purchased at the centre. If your laptop has a DVD drive you can use the films as an adjunct to

a visit to the area.

Before visiting the Memorial to the Missing it is possible to see the intricacy of Lutyens' design in a perfect scale replica of the memorial in the entrance lobby of the visitor centre.

A beautiful scaled model replical of the Memorial to the Missing in the entrance of the centre. MICHAEL STEDMAN

Above & below: Various stands and exhibits on show inside the new Thiepval Visitor Centre. MICHAEL STEDMAN

I am grateful to Sir Frank Sanderson of the Thiepval project for his permission to use some materials within this guidebook. All the graphics at the centre were produced by M2 Graphics of London whose expertise was second to none. In particular I should like to mention David Edgell, Tony Lyons, Duncan Youel and Lynnette Eve. I have also been inspired by the team of historians whose work created the displays. Those historians were Michael Barker, Nigel Cave, Professor Peter Simkins and myself. I think I can do no better than to quote from the few words which I wrote in the Visitor Centre guidebook:

Thiepval is both an inspiration and an education to all but it is the next generation who will need to learn most from this place. I believe this centre will help to inspire the young men and women of today with both a love of history and the need to ensure that its many lessons are not lost or wasted. Above all, as you walk around this place, I hope you will remember the sacrifice and human cost which were a part of this terrible war.

The ownership and management of the Centre has now devolved upon the Conseil Général of the Somme. The centre is manned by English speaking staff on site. Opening hours, seven days a week, are 0900 to 1700 November – April, and 1000 to 1800 May – October. The only closure will be around Christmas and the New Year. The address is:

8 rue de l'Ancre, 80300 THIEPVAL, France.
The telephone number is **00.33. (0) 3.22.74.60.47.**

TOUR OF THE AREA

A GENERAL TOUR OF THE AREA TO FAMILIARIZE YOURSELF WITH THE MAIN FEATURES AROUND THIEPVAL.

This section provides a general tour, too long to undertake except by car or coach and designed to make you familiar with the main features and sights found within the area. It will allow you to develop a more detailed understanding of particular locations.

This is suitable for all cars and most coaches. If you stop at all the suggested locations this may take three hours to complete. I suggest that you make use of the relevant IGN maps. The Green series 1:100,000 Laon – Arras sheet will suffice, but more detail can be gleaned by making use of the Blue series 1:25,000 sheets, the three most useful being 2407 east west with 2408 west to cover the Albert and Aveluy areas. However, the map below will help if you have been unable to obtain the IGN sheets.

A suitable starting point is the town of Albert. Leave on the Ameins Road, the D929, but turn right 250 metres from the town centre onto the D938 heading north-west in the direction of Bouzincourt. West of Bouzincourt are the many billet villages familiar to the troops who served here. During 1915 and 1916 Bouzincort lay some miles behind the British lines and housed many divisional command and communication posts as well as a main dressing station and the major medical evacuation facilities which were prepared prior to the Big Push of July 1916. There is a communal cemetery and extension here, the village being used as a Field Ambulance Station from early 1916 to February 1917. However, the views from Bouzincourt are restricted by the terrain and a far better prospect can be obtained by turning right and leaving the village on the D20 Bouzincourt to Aveluy road. One and a half kilometres along that road lies an area of higher ground with fine views in the direction of Thiepval and over Albert. It was along this dusty track, and on a little path running out of Martinsart, that many of the casualties from 1st July's fighting at Thiepval were evacuated. Bouzincourt Ridge British Military Cemetery can be reached along the sunken lane to the right which leaves the Bouzincourt Road here. This sunken lane is not passable by car except with great caution and in mid summer. A pleasant walk of 800 metres takes you to the cemetery entrance gateway, whose design mirrors that of the Thiepval memorial arch which can be seen clearly in the distance. This cemetery contains 708 graves.

Continue eastwards and downhill towards Aveluy, still along the D20. During 1916 the village of Aveluy

was in British hands, only to be captured by the Germans in late March 1918. Aveluy village contains a British military cemetery built as an extension to the village's communal graveyard. The cemetery was used by the British Army from August 1915 until March 1917. It was constructed next to a Field Ambulance and contains

ROUTE MAP TOUR OF ALBERT - THIEPVAL AREA

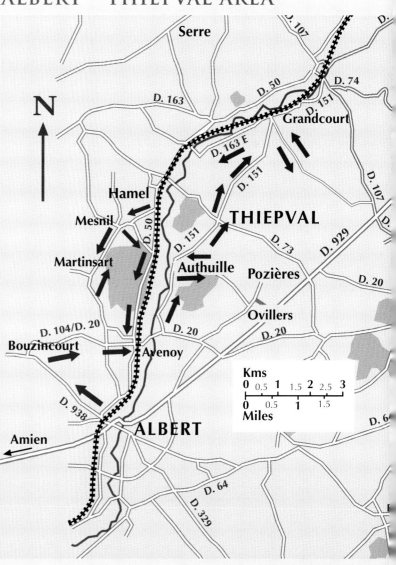

the graves of many men who died of wounds there. The cemetery can be reached by crossing over the cross roads at the D50, and thence over the railway bridge before entering the wide junction keeping to the left in the direction of Authuille. Turn sharp left just beyond this junction and the cemetery is 150 metres along the lane on your left. Return to the D20 and continue eastwards toward Authuille. As you leave Aveluy the road slopes down towards Ancre. The river has been canalized here. On your left was one of the iron bridges constructed by the British engineers to carry traffic towards Thiepval and which was only demolished during 1995. At the 'T' junction 300 metres away is the left turn towards Authuville. This is the notorious Crucifix Corner which was an important forward dump and water cart filling point from which hundreds of wiring parties were sent up to reinforce the British defences on the Ovillers ridge and in front of the Leipzig Redoubt. Today the corner is marked by a vehicle breaker's yard within the quarry behind the crucifix. In 1916 the quarry housed shelters in dugouts under the east face of the chalk walls. Above the quarry were important series of trenches known as the Bridgehead Defences. From the quarry an important trench tramway ran northwards alongside the east side of the Authuille Road.

Turn left at Crucifix Corner, along the D151 in the direction of Authuille. Cut into the roadside 100 metres on your right are a series on gun pits used by artillery units during the bombardment of Thiepval and nearby locations during the last week of June 1916. The right hand side of the road was the location to the trench tramway. Soon, as the road rounds a spur of higher ground, you will see a valley to your right. This is Blighty Valley, along which a well maintained grass path leads to the British Cemetery which contains over 1,000 graves, almost half of which contain casualties from the 1st July's fighting. Behind the cemetery is the embarkment within which the dugouts housing 14th and 97th Brigade HQs were established prior to the 1st July attacks across Leipzig Redoubt. Running along the valley floor the tramway then rose into the woods to a loading platform in the middle of the woodland area.

Above Blighty Valley Cemetery lies Authuille Wood (Bois de la Haie) which is the subject of a separate walking tour. If you prefer you can delay your visit to Blighty Valley until you choose to walk the Authuille Wood tour.

Return to the road and continue north along the D151, running parallel to the River Ancre. On your left, as the road rises slightly on the approach to Authuille, is the village communal cemetery. In 1915 many French soldiers had been buried here but those remains have since been removed to the large French National Cemetery on the D938 Peronne Road outside the town of Albert, to where all the small French battlefield cemeteries in this area were concentrated. The slopes behind Authuille's communal cemetery, above the River Ancre, were known as The Black Horse shelters, roughly 150 metres south of the village. Because of the convex nature of the slope they were generally free from small-arms and artillery fire. The Black Horse road ran down through Aveluy Wood and across the Ancre marshes, thence over the causeway/bridge due west of the village cemetery. It was within the Black Horse shelters that many men of 14th Brigade took refuge before their march south and the abortive attempt to cross Leipzig Redoubt on the morning of 1st July 1916.

Enter the village of Authuille and drive past the distinctive village church. In front of you, in the triangle of the grassy embankment above the junction, are two memorials. The longest standing is the village war memorial which includes the name of Boromee Vaquette, the first Frenchman from the village to be killed here, as well as others whose descendants still live and work within the village. In a privileged position beside this is the recently established Salford Pals' memorial. This records the close links with the village which the three Salford Pals' Battalions, the 15th, 16th and 19th Lancashire Fusiliers, established throughout the first six months of 1916.

Take a sharp right turn up the slope opposite the village and Salford Pals' memorials in the direction of

British cemetery in Authuille. MICHAEL STEDMAN

the Lonsdale Cemetery. This road is not really suitable for large coaches in that turning round to return is not easy, although cars and mini buses will find quite satisfactory turning points. At the summit, to your left can be seen Leipzig Salient and the Granatloch amongst the prominent group of trees. A little past the summit is the Lonsdale Cemetery near to which a number of British front line trenches can still be seen with care. This area will be dealt with in detail during the Authuille Wood area tour. Turn round and return to Authuille along the same road, at the foot of which turn right onto the D151 again. Keep to the right at the fork outside Authuille.

You are now driving along the Authuille to Thiepval road. On your left is Thiepval Wood, or Bois d'Authuille on your IGN map. This was the most important assembly point prior to the British attack on Thiepval on 1st July. Just to the left of Thiepval Wood can be seen Caterpillar Copse, either side of which ran two important communication trenches, Paisley Avenue on the north and Hamilton Avenue on the south. On your right, due east of Caterpillar Copse, lies the Thiepval Memorial to the Missing. As you pass the boundary fence of the Memorial and approach the church you will see a large farm on the left of the road, this is the site of the pre-war château. Many of today's visitors are under the impression, falsely, that the Memorial was built upon the site of the original château.

The cross roads next Thiepval church is a fine vantage point. The buildings shown on trench and pre-1914 maps to the north-west of the church have been obliterated, leaving an uninterrupted view today. Look down the Thiepval Road towards Thiepval Wood. The land to the left of the Thiepval Road is the old chateau's gardens, with which a circular driveway once provided pleasant walks an opportunity for quiet conversation. By late 1915 part of the British front line was located on this driveway with Thiepval Points North and South as small salients jutting towards the north and south of the chateau's buildings. At the bottom of those gardens Hammerhead Sap ran along the foot of the chateau's property, jutting out into No Man's Land parallel to the lane which once lay in the valley in front of Thiepval Wood. During 1916, in the gardens, two small stands of trees provided a landmark. On the German front line lay Diamond Wood. 200 metres forward of the British lines, lay Oblong Wood, to which a sap had been constructed from the British front line at the door of the gardens.

Just to the left of the Thiepval Road, 800 metres distant from the church and adjacent to Thiepval Wood, you can see Connaught Cemetery. Connaught marks the British front line positions facing Schwaben Redoubt. It was from this north-eastern face of Thiepval Wood that the Ulstermen debouched on the morning of 1st July. On the right of the road, immediately opposite Connaught, a path leads to Mill Road Cemetery, which is situated on the German forward lines just west of Schwaben Redoubt. Beyond both cemeteries lies the Ulster Tower which is built on the German front line above the slope running down to the Ancre, between St Pierre Division

and Hamel. The Thiepval Wood area is also the subject of a separate walking tour.

Running in an easterly direction from the church is the D73 leading to Pozières. Mouquet Farm can easily be reached from this road.

You can now move towards Schwaben Redoubt by driving north out of Thiepval along the D151. 400 metres along the road out of the village is the communal cemetery. Keep right here and continue slightly uphill until you reach *la Grande Ferme* in another 600 metres. This cluster of buildings is the site of *Feste Schwaben*, the highest point in the vicinity of Thiepval and the most imposingly fortified of the redoubts along the German front in this sector. Thiepval and the Schwaben Redoubt fell to the 18th Division during September and October 1916. Continue along the D151 past *la Grande Ferme* where you can see Battery Valley on your left (Vallee Caronnesse on your IGN map). Stop at the cross roads on the spur above Grandcourt (R.15.a.8.6. on your trench map). This is the eastern limit of this guide and on your right is the Stump Road, which is not suitable for coaches, leading up to *Feste Staufen* and *Feste Zollern*. Because those areas are isolated you may wish to explore them in detail now.

After returning to the D151 from Stump Road turn right and drive down the slope into Grandcourt. Turn left and then left again to take the D4151 (marked D163E on IGN 1:25,000 maps) travelling west in the direction of St Pierre Division. Ignore the right turn marked for Beaucourt and head straight on to St Pierre Division's few buildings. During November of 1916 this area was the scene of the most hideous fighting within the valley of the Ancre. The onset of wet weather and the inability of the marshes to drain the area meant that troops were forced to fight and endure the most unspeakably horrible conditions. Continue along the road through St Pierre Division, with its maze of subterranean defences which were entered through the huge embankment to your left, until the junction with the D73 Thiepval road. Turn right and across the Ancre and then the level crossing, beyond which you should turn left onto the D50. This will take you to Hamel. This was on the left of the 36th Division's lines. From the Mesnil Ridge, above Hamel, three important communication trenches ran down into Hamel. The most northerly was Esau Alley, coming down from Fort Jackson (Q.16.d,0,0), then Charles Avenue and lastly Jacob's Ladder, a particularly dangerous trench in that it was overlooked and enfiladed by fire from Schwaben and above Beaucourt. Staying on the D50 pass through the village of Hamel beyond which, just after the British Military Cemetery, you should take the right fork towards Mesnil along the C7. As you drive up the slope you are moving parallel to Jacob's Ladder, which ran 200 yards to the right of the road as you proceed uphill. As you entre Mesnil you will come to the D174. A right turn here will be of special interest for those people following the story of the 36th Division's Ulstermen for whom it is worth noting that north of Mesnil, halfway to Auchonvillers along a track not accessible to coaches, lies Mensil Ridge Military Cemetery. This cemetery contains the graves of many soldiers from the 36th Division killed during the period from their arrival in late 1915 through to July 1916.

From Mesnil you should also make a small diversion to the village of Martinsart, one mile to the south-west along the C7. Martinsart was the scene of a disaster which befell the 13th Royal Irish Rifles two days before the opening of the Somme offensive when one platoon of the battalion was devastated by the horrific effects of a single shell. Martinsart was important to the Ulsters as the origin of the tramway which maintained supplies to their Thiepval positions. It was also, quite extraordinarily in view of the size of the village, the permanent billet for five battalions of Ulstermen! During the final week-long bombardment these five battalions were sent further back to Varennes, Leavillers, Hedauville and Forceville in order to avoid the expected German bombardment of Martinsart. In fact no substantial bombardment fell upon Martinsart until after the start of the Ulster's attack. Just south of Martinsart, on the D129 heading towards Aveluy, you will be able to find Martinsart's military cemetery from where, due east, you can obtain good views towards Aveluy Wood. The fourteen men killed by that fateful shell are buried within the first graves dug within the cemetery. Now return to Mesnil.

Pass through the village and continue towards Mensil's eccentric chateau, in a south-easterly direction, downhill along the D174 towards Authuille. Here, in front of the chateau but on the left side of the road, you can stand at the site of 'Brock's Benefit' from which Brigadier General H.J. Brock of the 36th Division was able to monitor the effect of his artillery on the German's Thiepval defences opposite. While you are at Brock's Benefit, looking down the D174, take note that on your right, behind the chateau, is Aveluy Wood. To your left, across the valley of the Ancre in the direction of the Thiepval memorial, is Thiepval Wood. In a line directly between Mensil and Thiepval Wood lay the *Passerelle de Magenta*, across which were constructed two important causeways, north and south, each capable of carrying infantry in fours and 18-pounder gun limbers with their teams. Thiepval Wood provided cover for two branches of the trench tramway which was constructed during the early summer of 1916. One branch ran along the east face of the wood and served the requirements of the 36th Division there. The other branch ran along the southern edge of Thiepval Wood, between Paisley Avenue trench and Caterpiller Copse, and served the 32nd Division. At the foot of the slope turn right onto the D50 in the direction of Albert. After 100 metres you will see Aveluy (Lancashire Dump) Cemetery on your left. This dates from mid summer 1916 and was used by units and Field Ambulances until early 1917 and later during 1918. Here, within the confines of the woodland, you can easily visualize the vital cover afforded by the trees. It was possible to assemble a division of troops within the woods without their being seen from the Thiepval ridge. The wood was therefore crucial in the processes of

supplying the munitions and material needed by British units operating in the Thiepval sector. To help in this task the trench tramway had been built which originated in the valley between Aveluy Wood and Martinsart village, just below the military cemetery on the D129, and terminated in Thiepval Wood. The tramway rose from its start near Martinsart (54.d.S.E.4.W.4.a.0,0) through the southern end of Aveluy Wood and then ran alongside the Albert to Hamel Road to a siding next to Lancashire Dump. From here the tramway ran east through a tunnel built under the main railway track and on towards the Ancre (which it crossed at the site of the present day river bridge at the Hotel des Pecheurs). As you drive back along the D50 through Aveluy Wood, towards Albert, you will be able to see glimpses of the view over the Ancre valley to your left. Below the road lies the main line railway cutting. Between that railway and the road are a vast network of trenches, many of which were constructed during 1918. You should be aware that this part of the wood is oft frequented by hunters who use traps and shotguns in pursuit of their Sunday dinner. Make sure you don't end up on their plate like the quail and venison!

From here, in Aveluy Wood, it is just five minutes by car back into Albert by which time you should have a clear mental picture of the Thiepval area.

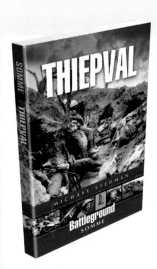

THE PALS BATTALIONS SERIES

ACCRINGTON PALS - *William Turner*

The Accrington Pals were the most famous of the Pals battalions. Based upon research in local and national archives and interviews with the battalion's handful of survivors, their many relations and descendants, Accrington Pals contains a great number of unpublished eye-witnessed accounts and photographs.

ISBN: 0 85052 360 5 • **Price: £17.95** • Pbk

BARNSLEY PALS - *Jon Cooksey*

In response to Kitchener's famous call for a million volunteers, local communities raised entire battalions for service on the Western Front. Their experience was all too frequently tragic, as men who had known each other all their lives, had worked, volunteered and trained together encountered the first full fury of modern battle on the Somme in July 1916.

ISBN: 0 85052 523 3 • **Price: £14.95** • Pbk

BIRMINGHAM PALS - *Terry Carter*

The City of Birmingham formed three battalions with over 3,000 local volunteers. Birmingham Pals covers the full range of human experience in war - the highest courage and bravery, the misery and tedium of trench life, the exhilaration, terror and slaughter involved in 'going over the top'. Above all, it is a tale of comradeship, which, for many survivors, was to last a life time.

ISBN: 0 85052 547 0 • **Price: £17.95** • Pbk

BRADFORD PALS - *David Raw*

Published June
In the early days of the First World War two volunteer Pals Battalions were raised in Bradford and this is their remarkable story. David Raw's account is based on memoirs, letters, diaries, contemporary newspaper reports, official records and archives, and it is illustrated with many maps and previously unpublished photographs.

ISBN: 1 84415 370 3 • **Price: £16.99** • Hbk

CHESHIRE BANTAMS - *Stephen McGreal*

Published August
Raised in Birkenhead in 1914, the Bantams were unique as the average height of the volunteers was a mere five foot! Previously denied the opportunity to serve, these men seized this chance to join up. As a result the battalions comprised working class men from all over Britain. The Bantams fought on the Somme where casualties were so severe that by 1917 the Division effectively ceased to exist.

ISBN: 1 84415 387 8 • **Price: £19.99** • Hbk

HULL PALS - *David Bilton*

In response to Kitchener's famous call for a million volunteers, local communities raised entire battalions for the service on the Western Front. This book tells their inspiring story of sacrifice and gallantry under appaling conditions. Hull Pals contains a great number of hitherto unpublished eye-witnessed accounts and photographs.

ISBN: 0 85052 634 5 • **Price: £18.95** • Pbk

LEEDS PALS - *Laurie Milner*

This is the story of the Leeds Pals, which by the war's end in 1918, were described as having been 'four times wiped out to the end'. It is a story which traces, in great and fascinating detail, the raising and training of the battalion in and around Leeds and their heavy losses on the Somme. Based upon the accounts of survivors, private and official letters and papers, it is a story of great courage.

ISBN: 0 85052 335 4 • **Price: £17.95** • Pbk

MANCHESTER PALS - *Michael Stedman*

The Manchester battalions were composed of middle-class men whose experience before the war years was within the commercial, financial and manufacturing interests which formed the foundations of Edwardian Manchester's life and prosperity. The Manchester Pals were part of one of the few successful actions in the battle of the Somme, taking the villages of Montauban and Mametz.

ISBN: 1 84415 046 1 • **Price: £19.95** • Hbk

SWANSEA PALS - *Bernard Lewis*

This is the first full history of the Battalion covering early recruiting for the battalion in the Swansea area and its subsequent training in Swansea, Rhyl and Winchester, prior to departure some 1200 strong in December 1915 for the Western Front. As part of the 38th Welsh Division it participated in the attack on Mametz Wood on the Somme.

ISBN: 1 84415 252 9 • **Price: £14.99** • Pbk

SHEFFIELD PALS - *Ralph Gibson*
& Paul Oldfield Published June

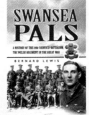

On the 10th September 1914, the City of Sheffield officially raised its own battalion. Just three and a half years later in February 1918, the Battalion was disbanded, never to be reformed. Sheffield Pals covers the raising of the battalion, training, the battle of the Somme and aftermath. With a unique selection of photographs, this book is a tribute to the men who served in the Sheffield City Battalion.

ISBN: 1 84415 423 8 • **Price: £19.99** • Hbk

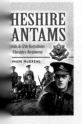

'The men were knocked down in droves as they began to bunch and searched in vain for gaps in the German wire. The Sheffield Pals in their turn wandered to their right, a few finding a gap in the wire and surged into the front line trench.'

THE BATTLE FOR SERRE 1ST JULY 1916

The 31st Division, comprising three brigades of infantry of which ten battalions were recruited from Yorkshire (eleven if the Pioneer battalion is included), one from Lancashire and one from Durham, was part of Fourth Army commanded by Lieutenant General Sir Henry Rawlinson. His Army would fight the initial stages of the first British Battle of the Somme.

By Jack Horsfall & Nigel Cave

This article was extracted from Jack Horsfall & Nigel Cave's book, *Serre - Battleground Series* and is reproduced here by permission of Pen and Sword Books Ltd.

The origins of the Battle of the Somme, its strategic objectives and the complications created by the planning of a huge offensive by two allies are not part of this book. Let it suffice to say that the planning was meticulous, the efforts to provide an infrastructure for the rear areas to cope with the massive influx of men and material extraordinary, with the most comprehensive system ever so far arranged for the evacuation of the wounded. Yet the planning was often flawed, the scheme, once launched, could not be easily changed and the extent of the casualties overwhelmed the evacuation system, at least on the first day of this battle that went on for over four and a half months.

The division at Serre was at the northern point of the whole fifteen mile British offensive line; it would sweep around in an arc of ninety degrees and provide a shield from German attacks from the north as the rest of the army pivoted upon it and swept the Germans off their heights, out of the Ancre and beyond, with the cavalry ready to follow in hot pursuit. This northernmost division would have one hour and fifty minutes to perform its task and to establish its shield, and end up facing north, retaining its link with 48th (South Midland) Division to its left.

31st Division's right flank ran along the front of the four small copses, with the most northerly one, John, precisely at the division's – indeed the army's – pivot point. Beyond this copse there would be no battle other than a diversionary attack at Gommecourt, two miles further to the north. The northerly barricade that the division was to create was to be 3,000 yards long, stretching eastwards from John Copse.

The task given to the division involved a most complex military manoeuvre, all of which had to be achieved under the fire of an extremely able enemy which had had many months both to fortify the ground on which it stood and also to know the ground over which its enemy was coming, and to register (that is to establish accurately the range) targets for its artillery. The infantry of 31st Division was composed entirely of 'Pals'.

The Pals phenomenon, one feels, could only have come about in Great Britain. This was a country that had for many years, perhaps for good reason, neglected its army to the benefit of its navy. When entanglement in continental war came about in 1914, the machine was totally inadequate to produce the sort of manpower that the new War Minister, Kitchener, realized would be required to win that war. In a characteristic solution, men from many towns and cities (chiefly in the great northern industrial towns), were recruited under local

Recruits for the 1st Barnsley Pals (13th Battalion York & Lancaster Regiment) on parade without uniforms. These men were mainly drawn from the colleries in town areas.

Privat Frank Lindley 2nd Barnsley Pals recalled; 'I'll always remember the Sheffielders with their hankerchiefs stuffed up their sleeves and wristwatches flashing in the sun. They were the elite of Sheffield. We were the ragged arse battalion but they were the coffee and bun boys.'

City Battalion men of the 12th Battalion. York & Lancaster Regiment at their camp on the moors outside Sheffield. Most of them would have been office workers.

control, generally the town councils. They were trained in local parks, housed in municipal buildings, clothed and equipped by the town and often officered by local worthies and a number of 'dugouts' from previous conflicts, most notably the Boer War at the turn of the century. After some months they were inspected by the War Office, found to be 'efficient' and taken over by the army, the town being compensated for its expenditure.

Although they were given battalion numbers according to the regiment to which they were attached (with the addition of 'Service' to their battalion number) the vast majority retained their nicknames – Hull Commercials, Sheffield City, Barnsley, Bradford, Accrington and Leeds Pals. After a period of training, often on Salisbury Plain, they were despatched overseas, some to Egypt, but most to France. Even those that went to Egypt, like the 31st Division, soon returned to France. Many of them had been in the army for eighteen months or more before they fought on 1st July – a long time to be in training. But they were all so inexperienced, as were their staff

OFFICIAL HISTORY MAP SHOWING THE DISPOSITION OF 31ST DIVISION ON THE EXTREME NORTH OF THE SOMME ATTACK

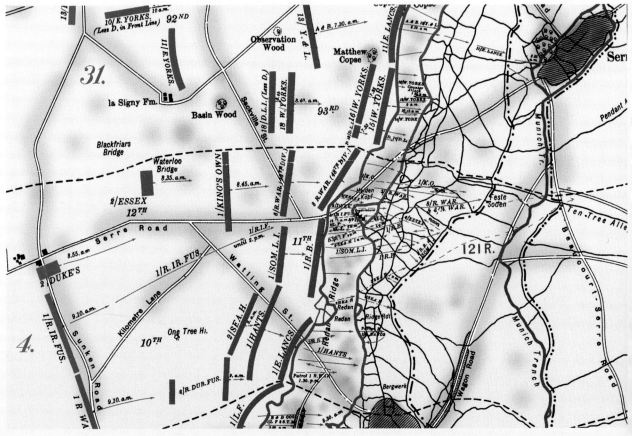

officers, their artillery and their support arms a striking contrast to the Germans opposite, with a war machine based on a complex and intensive conscription programme that had existed ever since the foundation of the Second Reich in 1870.

To the left of 31st Division, the 48th would stage diversionary fire on their front, though they 'lent' half of 143rd Brigade to their neighbour. These two battalions, Territorials of the Royal Warwickshire Regiment (1/6th and 1/8th) were put at the joint between 31st Division and 4th Division to its immediate south, or right.

From the corner of John Copse down to the right hand man of 1/8th Warwicks was a front line of 2,000 yards, with fifteen battalions confronting this insignificant little ridge top village. Four of these battalions were from Hull, comprising 92nd Brigade, which would be in reserve on the day, 800 to 1,500 yards behind the front line, entrenched on the Hebuterne-Colincamps Plain and just over the western edge of the shallow valley in the battle arena. In that valley, on both sides of it, were 93rd and 94th Brigades, those of 31st Division that would attack.

From north to south, the first 800 yards of front ran along the eastern edge of the four copses, with the remainder of the division's front being in the open, 300 yards above the valley floor.

In the front line, starting from John Copse, were half the Barnsley men of 14/Y&L, then Sheffield City men (12/Y&L). Beyond them were the Accrington Pals (11/East Lancs) and on their right were the Leeds Pals (15/West Yorks) who were adjacent to the Warwicks. In the front line trench and the five deep saps cut from it and under No Man's Land were strong elements from the four companies of 12/KOYLI, Miners and Pioneers' from Leeds.

Behind these front line troops, again commencing from the north, in company waves of 100 yards distance, were the other half of 14/Y&L. 1st Barnsley Pals (13/Y&L) were to the rear of the Lancashire men from Accrington. To the right of them were 16/West Yorks from Bradford, in trenches to the rear of the Leeds Pals. The right hand man of the Leeds Pals could shake hands with the left hand man of 1/8th Warwicks. A hundred yards behind 16/West Yorks were their fellow Bradford men of 18/West Yorks. Behind both of these battalions were 18/DLI, but D Company of the Geordies had been placed further forward, on the right flank of 16/West Yorks. All the battalions of both brigades were staggered in hundred yard waves throughout and on both sides of the shallow valley. The dispositions were planned to take into account the nature of the manoeuvre that was expected of the division - the fewest troops at the point of the pivot, the weight of manpower increasing towards the end of the sweeping arm.

The westward edge of the valley was topped with a long track running due north from the ruins of the large La Signy Farm to a point 500 yards behind John Copse, where it dipped down into the flat land that lay before Hebuterne. Roughly half way along this track was Observation Copse, in front of which a ten foot deep dugout had been made to hold the brigade headquarters, giving the staff a view over the whole of the division's battlefield and also of their objective, the ruins of Serre. They could also appreciate the external strength of the German position, approximately 800 yards away, its trenches and barbed wire forest. The artillery would doubtless put paid to that. Of the extent of the German underground position they had only the haziest notion.

To the left rear of this position, about 500 yards away, was Staff Copse (both these names a direct translation from the original French trench maps). Directly behind Luke Copse, also sitting alongside the track, were the ruins of the large Toutvent Farm, reduced to a pile of bricks and strewn detritus. The valley below was interlaced with trenches, all given names such as Monk, Eczema, Rob Roy, Nairne, Copse, Flag and Campion to name but a few. From these trenches long communication trenches were dug out of the valley, stretching westwards. Some of them had entrances 2,000 yards away, close to the road running north from Colincamps to Hebuterne. Coming south eastwards from the ridge top track near La Signy Farm was a long trench, Sackville Street. It was effectively 31st Division's right hand boundary, though it passed through both battalions of the Royal Warwicks. Just beyond its commencement a military police post was set up at Red

Men of the Royal Warwicks moving up to the front of the Somme.

Cottage to control the movements of troops in and out of the battle area. In front of the farm was a small round wood sprouting out of a hollow, Basin Wood. A large pit had been dug there to accommodate the dead from the forthcoming battle, a daunting and sobering sight for troops moving up for the attack.

31st Division had arrived in the Serre area in April 1916 on its arrival in France from a time spent in Egypt guarding the Suez Canal approaches. The base was about five miles away to the west around Bus-les-Artois. Most of its 15,000 men would have made constant treks in and out of the front, taking their turn to hold the line, to dig and improve the position, to rebury many of the hastily covered French dead as they did so and to make the trench system one from which a major attack could be launched.

They had two months to familiarize themselves with this new territory; two months when they faced an enemy for the first time; two months to learn their task in the forthcoming 'Big Push'. They had very little idea of what the German line looked like, though there were maps and aerial photographs from which to work. To spend too long gazing eastwards was to invite retribution from an alert enemy.

The German opposition had been at Serre for twenty months now. Unlike the British who were forced to move troops from sector to sector, especially as the army mushroomed in size, the Germans were almost static. They had built their defences with care and consideration; their men had ample opportunity to know exactly how to react to attack. They had time to make their men as comfortable as possible – a contrast to their adversary.

The Germans could also view the preparations the British were making, both from here and from the high ground which lay behind their front line. Their artillery was well concealed and could register the British positions; whilst much of the British artillery (the vast proportion of which was light and therefore short range) was often positioned on the open plain.

The battle was originally to start on 29th June; from

Hundreds of British guns were brought forward to bombard the German front line with the hope of breaking barbed wire defences.

Saturday 24th the artillery was going to batter the German defences into ruins, particularly the wire, and destroy the German defenders as effective fighting troops. Huge stock piles of ammunition had been brought forward (no easy task) and hundreds of guns would set about their task. Almost two thirds of these were field artillery, 18 pounders, whose main task was to destroy the barbed wire defences; over 300 howitzers would destroy machine gun posts and trenches, whilst the heaviest artillery was dedicated to destroying the deep, strong dugouts and underground barracks. Almost two million shells were fired along the front of the battle.

On the morning of 28th June the attack was postponed from Z day because of the restrictions imposed by the weather and the need for more work to be done on the wire. The attack was now to be launched at 7.30 a.m. on 1st July. The Germans sat and waited, seeing some of their defences smashed to ruin and suffering some, but surprisingly few, casualties. Their artillery bombarded the British positions – infantry and artillery, but the modest volume of this fire deceived

> The Germans sat and waited, seeing some of their defences smashed to ruin and suffering some, but surprisingly few, casualties.

Bois de Loyeast *Puisieux — au — M*

their enemy. The concealed batteries patiently waited for their moment.

During the evening of 30th June those battalions which had been detailed for the attack made their long march of five to seven miles into the trenches, across fields soaked in water and deep in the cloying mud of the Somme, entering crowded and narrow communications trenches whose floors were in a semi liquid condition. Caked in mud and tired out, the men got into their positions between 2 and 4 a.m., carrying their heavy loads of kit, emergency rations, spare ammunition and grenades, weapons, entrenching tools, wire cutters and often reels of barbed wire and other trench stores. But they were in a high state of anticipation, buoyed up at the thought that something was going to happen and encouraged by the ferocious sound of their artillery bombardment.

The four battalions of the East Yorks from Hull which had been holding the divisional front, patrolling, cutting wire and suffering casualties now withdrew out of the valley and beyond the La Signy-Touvent farms ridge, doubtless grateful to be spared the advance into the unknown in a few hours time. Two of their platoons remained with 18/DLI and seventy men went to the Accrington Pals as reinforcements. All knew what their task was in the carefully worked out plan; it was not so clear what was to happen if the plan went wrong.

31st Division had 110 minutes to establish their new defensive line from the moment that the attack commenced. It had to smash through four lines of deep German trenches and their thick barbed wire defences as well as overcoming the ten heavy machine guns of which they had limited knowledge. Bradford and Durham men on the right flank would have to advance 3,000 yards, with the outer flank having to hold Pendant Wood on the edge of Ten Tree Alley. The Royal Warwicks were to remove the Heidenkopf, the bulge in the German line and thereby ease their progress.

13 and 14/Y&L, 18/West Yorks and 18/DLI would then leapfrog as those who had gone ahead succeeded, consolidating positions and eliminating pockets of enemy resistance. They would be followed by the Hull brigade, whilst the Pioneers would connect German trenches to the British and effect emergency repairs. The

This diagram shows how deep the German bunkers were underground. Most were untouched by the seven day British artillery bombardment.

Germans would then be confronted by a well dug in division, elated by victory and prepared to deal with the inevitable counter-attacks from Puisieux.

At 6.30 a.m. the tempo of the British artillery increased, pouring fire on the German front; this lasted for fifty minutes. The weather had turned and the morning was clear and sunny. The Germans were clear about when the assault was going to happen from a variety of intelligence sources. They had managed to fly two balloons on 30th June and could appreciate fully the significance of the thousands of men that were flooding into the area. Their concealed artillery could now come into its own, launching a devastating fire on the

A panoramic view taken from Basin Wood, looking towards Serre, 12th April 1916. The 31st Division attacked from the left at the broken trees and advanced towards Serre on the right opposite.

comparatively soft British line, their guns already accurately laid for the task. The soldiers in the British front could only hug the trench walls and floors, suffer considerable casualties and wait for the off.

At 7.20 a.m. several things happened almost simultaneously. A great British mine was blown under Hawthorn Redoubt, about two miles to the south of Serre. At this moment the artillery barrage was lifted from the German front line – a clear and distinct signal to the battered Germans that now was the moment. Half companies of the five leading battalions climbed out of their trenches and ran forward 100 yards, lying down in front of the enemy wire and, with luck, out of range of German hand grenades. Stokes Mortars located in the saps that had been dug out just below the surface into No Man's Land now broke out from their overhead cover and began to let loose a barrage of 3,000 rounds onto the enemy front line trench. The final ingredient in this series of events was the letting off of an ineffectual smoke screen by 48th Division on the left, which drifted over onto the ground over which the Sheffield City battalion would advance.

Within a few minutes the British bombardment resumed its incessant fire, but concentrated further to the rear – this entirely the case for the heavier pieces of artillery. The 18 pounders, firing shrapnel, raised their sights to the German second line wire. At 7.25 a.m. the second half of the forward companies came out of their trenches and ran forward fifty yards, then lay down and awaited zero hour.

At 7.30 a.m. the whistles blew and the rest of the troops came out of their trenches to follow those already in No Man's Land; at a steady walk they headed for the gaps cut in the British wire and expected to be able to continue this progress across the, supposedly cut,

A re-enactment photograph portraying to the people back home in England how the attack would have looked. The reality was somewhat more horrific.

German wire and onto their objectives. Those in the following battalions began their advance to the front as well; they came in long files, the better to cross the many trenches between them and the Germans. As those on the left came forward they could see that the fog created by the smoke candles had drifted across our leading men and which now served to obscure the sight of their objectives.

The British barrage was now falling some hundreds of yards ahead of the leading infantry. The time scale of the advance was so tight that this, the forerunner of all creeping barrages, required the advancing infantry to maintain a steady speed to retain its protection. Already they were falling well behind.

The control of the conduct of the battle had now moved from the generals and even the battalion commanders, who were instructed to remain in the trenches in the first phase of the attack. This meant that it was junior officers and NCOs who were commanding the advance; and it was in just this category of soldier that Kitchener's Army was most deficient – the well tried and tested NCO who would have had time to train the junior officers. The men who had worked so hard to bring their battalions to a peak of battle readiness were now left – supposing they had survived – to watch their worst nightmare taking place in front of them in reality.

The artillery had tried very hard to carry out the vital part of the plan that was theirs. The shrapnel used for the most part by the field artillery was inadequate for the task of breaking up the German wire – it was not until the introduction of the instantaneous fuse that this particular problem was considerably overcome. A shortage of heavy calibre guns meant that many of the German underground shelters were untouched. Poor visibility in the early stages of the attack had not helped, nor had the excessively high proportion of dud rounds – perhaps as high as thirty per cent of all those fired. Only where the artillery was

The huge mine explosion at Hawthorne Ridge exploded two miles south of Serre under the German strongpoint known as the Hawthorne Redoubt.

heavy enough and of the right quality (on the British sector, only at Montauban) did it do its job and there the attack succeeded.

On the left of the attack, 14/Y&L were pushed to the right by the long range machine gun and artillery fire coming from the edge of Rossignol Wood, and in to the path of 12/Y&L. The men were knocked down in droves as they began to bunch and searched in vain for gaps in the German wire. The Sheffield Pals in their turn wandered to their right, a few finding a gap in the wire and surged into the front line trench. The Accringtons headed straight towards the village and were mown down by the sustained heavy machine-gun fire, yet some of these too found their way into the German line.

Further on the right the fortunes of 93rd Brigade were no better. The Leeds Pals were almost destroyed as a fighting force for that day before they even went over the top, and even those who had been in No Man's Land before zero hour failed to make any impact on the German line. Behind them the 1st Bradford Pals met a similar dreadful fate, making their approach over the very open ground in which they were entrenched. Within half an hour from the commencement of the assault over 2,000 men were down, either wounded in No Man's Land or dead. The German barbed wire had held the troops at bay and their artillery and machine guns had done the rest. Battalion commanders in the front could see that the battle was lost; whilst their beloved battalions could never again be what they had been. The Pals ideal was being destroyed before their eyes.

At 9.30 a.m. 18/DLI, 800 yards from the front line, stuck to their schedule even though they could see the awful disaster spread out before them. They went over the top in file, passing through 2nd Bradfords who had gone before them, with what was left of that battalion sheltering as best they could. They would get no further than the ruined forward trenches of 93 Brigade. On the left 1st Barnsley Pals had made a similar approach to the front, and also took their place in the disastrous scheme of things.

Meanwhile the surviving members of the detached element of 18/DLI, D Company, on the right hand edge of 1st Bradfords (16/West Yorks), continued to go forward into the smoke-shrouded battlefield, somehow surviving the numerous geysers of earth and shrapnel blown skywards by the enemy shells. The small metal plates made from pieces of biscuit tin and fastened to their back packs glistened in the sunshine and showed, to the observers in the rear and to the aircraft above, the Geordies' progress. Their progress was monitored as they moved further and further forward, diminishing in numbers as they went. It was reported that a dozen had penetrated the incredible distance of 2,000 yards until they reached the ridge top Pendant Copse and disappeared from view altogether – and forever.

31st Division's assault had come to a sanguinary halt; the fear now was that the Germans would counter-attack, and with enemy fire showing no sign of abating the Hull battalions of 92 Brigade were left in their reserve position.

Further south the Birmingham Territorials, 1/8th and 1/6th Warwicks, had also set off at 7.30 am. With the 1/8th in the lead they had swarmed over the slight rise in front of them, crossed the Serre Road and battered their way through the German fortress of the Heidenkopf. With 1/6th close behind them they fought their way for 1,000 yards into what should have been 31st Division's right boundary, 600 yards south of the village and crossed the junction of the German trench system at Munich Trench and Ten Tree Alley with the trench leading to Beaucourt. However the experienced Germans of the tough 169th Infantry Regiment, relieved of the necessity to defend Serre because of the destruction of 31st Division, rushed reinforcements to the area. The Warwicks were left in the air by the failure of the units on either side, those of the 31st and 4th Divisions. They had crossed two of the German lines and in just thirty minutes had reached the German third line of defence and were attempting to consolidate their gain. They were ejected and fought their way back in again on several occasions. Behind 1/6th Warwicks were trying to reach them but were being held up by the impenetrable German artillery fire, so that in the end only a few made it.

As the day progressed into afternoon supplies of bombs and ammunition began to run dangerously short. There was no alternative but to retire, leaving their dead and many of their wounded behind them. About ten hours after they had set off, they found themselves back where they had started, a shadow of their former selves. 1/8th had lost their CO, Lieutenant-Colonel E A Innes killed, and twenty-one out of the twenty-three officers who had gone over the top were killed or wounded, with only one taken prisoner because he was too badly injured to move. The total casualties of the battalion on that terrible day were 588. 1/6th had done only a little less badly. The CO, Lieutenant-Colonel W.H. Franklin, had been badly wounded and twenty-two other officers were killed or wounded, with 466 casualties for the whole battalion.

Of the four battalions of 93 Bde only 18/DLI, badly damaged as they were, had the ability to form a defence line, 400 yards behind the dead and wounded of the Leeds Pals who lay where they had been at 7.30 a.m. The two Bradford Pals battalions were equally wrecked. By 11 a.m. the brigade's sector was quiet save for some desultory German shelling, but although the sound of battle had gone it was replaced by the heart rending cries of hundreds of wounded men. For those who were not too badly injured, attempts to crawl back to their line was likely to result in sudden death at the hands of alert German snipers. In the trenches themselves the survivors struggled to rebuild their defences against an anticipated German counter-attack.

15/West Yorks, the Leeds Pals, had lost their CO wounded and out of action even before his men had gone over the top. His second in command, Stanley Neil, who had joined the Pals as a private, was killed along with nine other officers. 528 of their men were casualties.

GERMAN MAXIM 08-15 MACHINE GUN

SPECIFICATIONS

Calibre: 7.92mm

Muzzle velocity: 2,821 feet per second.

Sighting range: 2,200 yards.

Extreme range: (at 32 degrees) 4,400 yards.

Rate of fire: 400-500 rounds per minute.

Length (overall): 53 inches.

Barrel length: 28.35 inches.

Weight (filled with water): 43 pounds.

Water capacity: 5 pints.

Minimum height: 11 inches

ILLUSTRATION BY JON WILKINSON

With the German wire uncut, the British were held at bay in front of the trenches. This gave enemy machine gunners time to mow down waves of advancing troops.

The 1st Bradford Pals had lost their commander, Major C. S. Guyon, killed and had 515 casualties; the 2nd, who had never even got into No Man's Land, had 490 casualties and their CO, Lieutenant Colonel M.N. Kennard, killed. With the exception of D Coy, 18/DLI had also failed to reach No Man's Land; at the time of their relief on the night of 4th/5th July they had lost twelve officers and 406 other ranks.

C Coy and three platoons of B Coy from 12/KOYLI, the Pioneer battalion, had gone into action with 93 Bde. They had worked like demons in supporting and succouring their battered comrades. They made endless, blood-soaked, journeys back and forth with dead and wounded; they had redug, shored up and cleared collapsed trenches and dugouts; they had buried remains of men in the bottom of trenches and all the while had to do this under a rain of death falling about them. At mid-morning, because the Pioneers were the only battalion resembling a coherent force, they were ordered to act as infantry in face of the expected German attack and took up defensive positions along the division's right boundary in Sackville Street.

On the left of the division the 94th Brigade were also back from where they had started – a shattered remnant. Some had made it into the German first and second line trenches, and a few glistening plates had been spotted on the western edge of the village, indicating that some had got that far. They simply faded away. In February 1917 a handful of Accringtons and Sheffield men were found buried, unidentifiable, in the village. Doubtless they were simply cleared away by the garrison along with the rest of the debris of battle.

The commander of 11/East Lancs, the Accrington Pals' Lieutenant-Colonel W. Rickman had established his headquarters in C Sap, one of the five that had been dug out into No Man's Land. He found himself cut off from his brigade headquarters with all the telephone wires destroyed, despite the fact that they had been buried. Indeed they had been cut before the infantry battle had begun. His only means of communication was by runners, and few of these were to survive intact the 800 yards gap between the two headquarters. From his vantage point he had seen the waves of his men go past him, struggle up the slope towards the enemy line, many with their heads bent down as though walking into rain, and then they withered away as they fell victim to the German fire.

By midday the battle had, to all intents and purposes, ceased on this front. Lieutenant-Colonel Rickman gathered the survivors still behind the front line into some sort of defensive position on the eastern edge of the copse and with the help of the attached pioneers tried to move the hundreds of dead and wounded that lay about them. A few heroic stretcher bearers were moving about upright, the Germans permitted this mercy until some infantry began to fire at exposed Germans. Then all British troops in front of the German wire became targets.

The 1st Barnsley Pals (13/Y&L), whose task was to follow the Accringtons going for the centre of the village, had come down from the far side of the valley, across the ruined trenches whose bridges had all been blown away, and proceeded through the mud, shattered tree stumps and debris of Luke and Mark Copse, trying to get into No Man's Land. None of them managed to penetrate the German wire. Their task now was for those who remained to consolidate with the East Lancs survivors.

The Sheffield City Bbattalion faced a misfortune early

on. Their CO, Lieutenant-Colonel Crosthwaite, the only professional officer in the battalion and who had been badly wounded at Ypres, collapsed and had to be evacuated; although a blow, it is almost certain that his presence would have made no difference to what took place subsequently. The second-in-command, Major A Placket had his headquarters dugout in the middle of the shattered John Copse. He suffered the same fate of watching his battalion disintegrate, with only a very few men penetrating into the German second line. He soon became a casualty himself and was taken out of the line; it was left to a few young officers who were still on their feet (although all were wounded) to organize the survivors of Sheffield's pride, its City battalion.

The battalion on the extreme left of the whole British attack was 2nd Barnsley Pals (14/Y&L). In the front they only had two platoons, in position at the top, northern corner of John Copse, in Nairne Trench. Their task was to attack straight ahead and connect their trench to the captured German trenches so that there would be a new fire trench facing north, the beginnings of that 3,000 yard shield that was to be created by the division. The remainder of the battalion was in a series of trenches behind them on the western slope, with their commander, Lieutenant-Colonel Hulke, and his headquarters, in Roland Trench.

Like all the others, 2nd Barnsleys suffered casualties as it advanced at 7.30 a.m., in this case to follow on after the men from Sheffield. The CO decided at about 10 am that he would reinforce the two platoons whose job it was to create the new fire trench. Second Lieutenant Johnson was sent forward to Nairne Trench to help with the opening up of the Russian sap which had been dug by Barnsley miners into No Man's Land. (A Russian sap was a shallow tunnel which could easily be broken open to the surface, and thereby creating an instant trench under cover.) When he came to the location he could find nothing – no Nairne Trench, no sap, no survivors of the two platoons. There had been complete annihilation on this the steepest incline on the division's front.

94th Brigade's casualties mirrored 93rd's. The Accrington Pals lost 585; Lieutenant-Colonel Rickman survived almost the whole of the first day, but was knocked out by a shell blast in the evening. He survived and returned to his battalion, which he was still commanding in the summer of 1918. The Official History seems to have lost sight of this; in its terse few pages on the action at Serre, a footnote comments on his death in action! The Sheffield City Battalion had gone into action with 680 men in the front line; they suffered 512 casualties. Both the Barnsley Pals battalions lost over 400 men, whilst the divisional pioneers, 12/KOYLI had lost 192 men who were not there to fight with anything more offensive than a shovel had lost a third of their complement.

All thoughts of continuing the offensive against Serre had ended long before noon. The concern of the two brigadiers now lay in the intentions of the Germans, and the real possibility of a counter-attack.

The Germans did not attack; they had suffered damage themselves, they had defended their ground tenaciously and effectively, and in any case any attack across such shattered ground would have been difficult and possibly risky. They were content to reorganize themselves.

As darkness fell brave men went out into No Man's Land to try and recover as many of the wounded and dead as possible; this went on every night until the division was relieved on the short summer night of 4th July. The shattered survivors left the hell of their trenches before Serre and walked the miles back to Warnimont Wood whence they had set off with such high hopes the previous week, but which for many must have felt like a lifetime ago.

It was probably true of these battalions that everyone in these places knew someone who was a casualty at Serre. Although some battalions would suffer worse casualties in later actions, none had the same impact as this first great battle in which the infantry units of 31st Division had been involved; battalions built up over almost two years had lost so much of their manpower that they lost their character. It did not stop them, however, from becoming in many cases excellent fighting units.

The failure of 31st Division had very little impact on the battle, for only one division, and that on the extreme right, had achieved its first day objectives. This had captured a large hill top village (Montauban) after crossing another open but very wide valley and getting into their objective after three hours of fighting. The crucial difference lay not in the quality of command or soldiers but in the availability of heavier calibre guns, many of which belonged to the adjacent French army. As John Terraine has often pointed out, this was an artillery war.

When 31st Division got back to the Bus and the miserable huts in Warnimont Wood a final reckoning could be made; it had suffered 4,500 casualties.

'You must know that
I feel that every step
in my plan has been
taken with the Divine
help.'

Sir Douglas Haig to Lady Haig
before the battle.

'The news about
8 a.m. was not
altogether good.'

Sir Douglas Haig on 1st July.

'Our battalion
atttacked about 800
strong. It lost, I was
told in hospital,
about 450 the first
day, and 290 or so
the second.
I suppose it was
worth it.'

NCO of the 22nd Manchesters.

THE SOMME;
SUMMARY OF THE BATTLE

On 1st July 1916 a mainly volunteer British Army of 16 divisions in concert with five French divisions attacked entrenched German positions in the Department of the Somme in France. Over-reliance by the British on the destruction of enemy defences by preparatory artillery bombardment led to almost 60,000 British casualties on the first day and more than 400,000 before the fighting ended on 17th November 1916. The maximum advance made in all that time was six and a half miles. Total German casualties are estimated to have been about the same as the British and the French were almost 200,000.

By Valmai & Tonie Holt

This article was extracted from Major & Mrs Holt's *Concise Illustrated Battlefield Guide - The Western Front* and is reproduced here by permission of Pen and Sword Books Ltd.

OPENING MOVES

Few campaigns of recent history provoke such emotive British opinions as 'The Battle of the Somme'. Those who study the First World War tend to fall into two main camps: those who are anti-Haig and those who are pro-Haig. But there are those who move from one opinion to the other, according to the quality of debate. Was the C.-in-C. a dependable rock, whose calm confidence inspired all, whose far-seeing eye led us to final victory and who deserved the honours later heaped upon him? Or was he an unimaginative, insensitive product of the social and military caste system that knew no better: a weak man pretending to be strong, who should have been sacked? Doubtless the arguments will continue and more space than is available here is needed for a fair consideration, but there are some immovable elements: for instance the misjudgement concerning the artillery's effect upon the German wire and the appalling casualties on 1 July 1916.

Those casualties, while not sought for by the French, may well have been hoped for by them. At the end of 1915 the French and British planned for a joint offensive on the Somme, with the French playing the major role. Masterminded by Joffre, the plan was (as far as Joffre was concerned) to kill more Germans than their pool of manpower could afford. But when the German assault at Verdun drew French forces away from the Somme, the British found themselves with the major role, providing sixteen divisions on the first day to the French five.

It was to be the first joint battle in which the British played the major role and, in the opinion of some French politicians, not before time. There was a growing feeling that the British were not pulling their weight and a bloody conflict would stick Britain firmly to the 'Cause'. It was to be the first major battle for Kitchener's Army following their rush to the recruiting stations in the early days of the war.

It was also to be the first battle fought by General Haig as C.-in-C. There was a great deal riding on the outcome of the Battle of the Somme. The British plan was based upon a steady fourteen-mile-wide infantry assault, from Serre in the north to Maricourt in the south, with a diversionary attack at Gommecourt above Serre. One hundred thousand soldiers were to go over the top at the end of a savage artillery bombardment. Behind the infantry – men of the Fourth Army, commanded by General Rawlinson – waited two cavalry divisions under General Gough. Their role was to exploit success.

WHAT HAPPENED

The battle may be divided into five parts:

Part 1. The First Day	1st July
Part 2. The Next Few Days	2nd July +
Part 3. The Night Attack/The Woods	14th July +
Part 4. The Tank Attack	15th Sept
Part 5. The Last Attack	13th Nov

PART 1. THE FIRST DAY: 1ST JULY

At 0728 hours seventeen mines were blown under the German line. Two minutes later 60,000 British soldiers, laden down with packs, gas mask, rifle and bayonet, 200 rounds of ammunition, grenades, empty sandbags, spade and water bottles, clambered out of their trenches from Serre to Maricourt and formed into lines fourteen miles long. As the lines moved forward in waves, so the artillery barrage lifted off the enemy front line.

From that moment onwards it was a life or death race, but the Tommies didn't know it. They hadn't been 'entered'. Their instructions were to move forward, side by side, at a steady walk across No Man's Land. It would be safe, they were told, because the artillery barrage would have destroyed all enemy opposition. But the Germans were not destroyed. They and their machine guns had sheltered in deep dugouts, and, when the barrage lifted, they climbed out, dragging their weapons with them.

The Germans won 'the race' easily. They set up their machine guns before the Tommies could get to their trenches to stop them, and cut down the ripe corn of British youth in their thousands. As the day grew into hot summer, another 40,000 men were sent in, adding more names to the casualty lists. Battalions disappeared in the bloody chaos of battle, bodies in their hundreds lay around the muddy shell holes that pocked the battlefield.

And to what end this leeching of some of the nation's best blood? North of the Albert-Bapaume road, on a front of almost nine miles, there were no realistic gains at nightfall. VIII, X, and III Corps had failed. Between la Boisselle and Fricourt there was a small penetration of about half a mile on one flank and the capture of Mametz village on the other by XV Corps. Further south, though, there was some success. XIII Corps attacking beside the French took all of its main objectives, from Pommiers Redoubt east of Mametz to just short of Dublin Redoubt north of Maricourt.

The French, south of the Somme, did extremely well. Attacking at 0930 hours they took all of their objectives. *'They had more heavy guns than we did'*, cried the British generals, or *'The opposition wasn't as tough'*, or *'The Germans didn't expect to be attacked by the French'*. But whatever the reasons for the poor British performance in the north they had had some success in the south – on the right flank, beside the French.

PART 2. THE NEXT FEW DAYS: 2 JULY +

Other than the negative one of not calling off the attack, no General Command decisions were made concerning the overall conduct of the second day's battle. It was as if all the planning had been concerned with 1 July and that the staffs were surprised by the appearance of 2 July. Twenty-eight years later, on 7 June 1944, the day after D-Day, a similar culture enveloped the actions of the British 3rd Division in Normandy. Aggressive actions were mostly initiated at Corps level while Haig and Rawlinson figured out what policy they ought to follow. Eventually, after bloody preparation by the 38th (Welsh) Division at Mametz Wood, they decided to attack on the right flank, but by then the Germans had had two weeks to recover.

PART 3. THE NIGHT ATTACK/THE WOODS: 14 JULY +

On the XIII Corps front, like fat goalposts, lay the woods of Bazentin le Petit on the left and Delville on the right. Behind and between them, hunched on the skyline, was the dark goalkeeper of High Wood. Rawlinson planned to go straight for the goal. Perhaps the infantry general's memory had been jogged by finding one of his old junior officer's notebooks in which the word 'surprise' had been written as a principle of attack,

because, uncharacteristically, he set out to surprise the Germans and not in one, but in two, ways.

First, despite Haig's opposition, he moved his assault forces up to their start line in Caterpillar Valley at night. Second, after just a five-minute dawn barrage instead of the conventional prolonged bombardment, he launched his attack. At 0325 hours, 20,000 men moved forward. On the left were 7th and 21st Divisions of XV Corps and on the right 3rd and 9th Divisions of XIII Corps. The effect was dramatic. Five miles of the German second line were overrun. On the left Bazentin-le-Petit Wood was taken. On the right began the horrendous six-day struggle for Delville Wood. Today the South African Memorial and Museum in the wood commemorate the bitter fighting.

But in the centre 7th Division punched through to High Wood and with them were two squadrons of cavalry. Perhaps here was an opportunity for a major breakthrough at last. Not since 1914 had mounted cavalry charged on the Western Front but, when they did, the Dragoons and the Deccan Horse were alone. The main force of the cavalry divisions, gathered south of Albert, knew nothing about the attack. The moment passed, the Germans recovered, counter-attacked and regained the wood.

There followed two months of local fighting under the prompting of Joffre, but, without significant success to offer, the C.-in-C. began to attract increasing criticism. Something had to be done to preserve his image, to win a victory – or both.

It was: with a secret weapon – the tank.

PART 4. THE TANK ATTACK: 15 SEPTEMBER

Still very new and liable to break down, thirty-two tanks out of the forty-nine shipped to France in August assembled near Trônes Wood on the night of 14 September for dispersal along the front, and the following morning at 0620 hours, following a three-day bombardment, eighteen took part in the battle with XV Corps. Their effect was sensational. The Germans, on seeing the monsters, were stunned and then terrified. Nine tanks moved forward with the leading infantry, nine 'mopped up' behind. Barely over three hours later, the left hand division of XV Corps followed a solitary tank up the main street of Flers and through the German third line. Then Courcelette, too, fell to an infantry/tank advance.

The day's gains were the greatest since the battle began. But there were too few tanks and, after the initial shock success, the fighting once again degenerated into a bull-headed contest. The opportunity that had existed to use the tank to obtain a major strategic result had gone. Many felt that it had been squandered. Yet the tank had allowed 4th Army to advance and the dominating fortress of Thiepval finally fell on 26 September, helped, it was said, 'by the appearance of 3 tanks'. At last the British were on the crest of the Thiepval-Pozières-High Wood ridge. But Beaumont Hamel in the north still held out.

PART 5. THE LAST ATTACK: 13 NOVEMBER

At the northern end of the battlefield, seven divisions of the Reserve (5th) Army assaulted at 0545 hours on 13 November. Bad weather had caused seven postponements since the original date of 24 October. V Corps was north of the River Ancre and II Corps was south. The preparatory bombardment had been carefully monitored to see that the enemy wire had been cut, but this eminent practicality was offset by the stationing of the cavalry behind the line to exploit success. Apart from the overwhelming evidence of past battle experience that should have made such an idea absurd, the weather's effect on the ground alone should have rendered it unthinkable. The generals were as firmly stuck for ideas as any Tommy, up to his waist in Somme mud, was stuck for movement.

The attack went in with a shield of early morning dark and fog, the troops moving tactically from cover to cover. Beaumont Hamel and the infamous Y Ravine were taken by the 51st Highland Division and their kilted Highlander Memorial stands there today in memory of that achievement. Fred Farrell, the official artist attached to the Divisional HQ, sketched in detail the taking of the main German position at Y Ravine, identifying the men involved. The drawing is included in a collection published by T. C. and E. C. Jack in 1920. Fighting went on for several more days, and 7,000 prisoners were taken – though Serre did not fall. But at last enough was enough.

The attack was stopped and the Battle of the Somme was over.

THE BATTLEFIELD TOUR

There are more than 100 sites of particular interest to be seen on the Somme battlefield of 1916 – excluding those associated with the Kaiser's Offensive of 1918. Here we have selected those places whose names or memorials feature in the top requests made to us over the years.

See map on page 74.

[A more detailed tour can be made using our Major & Mrs Holts' Battlefield Guide to the Somme with our Battle Map of the Somme].

• **The Route:** The tour begins in Albert, visits the Golden Madonna and the Somme '14-'18 Museum; Bapaume Post CWGC Cemetery; la Boisselle – Tyneside Memorial Seat, the Lochnagar Mine Crater, the 19th (Western) and 34th Divisional Memorials; Contalmaison – McCrae's Bn Monument; Mametz Wood – Harry Fellows' grave, Flat Iron Copse CWGC Cemetery, 38th (Welsh) Division Dragon Memorial; Longueval – Caterpillar Valley CWGC Cemetery, Bristol's Own Cross, Pipers' Memorial, the South African Memorial, Museum and CWGC Cemetery at Delville Wood; High Wood – Cameron Highlanders & Black Watch, 47th (London) Division, 20th Bn RF Tree and Glasgow Highlanders' Memorials, London CWGC Cemetery; Courcelette Canadian Memorial; Pozières – Australian Windmill and Tank Memorials, Tommy Café recreated trenches, Australian 1st Division Memorial and Gibraltar Bunker; Thiepval – Visitor & Education Centre, Memorial to the Missing of the Somme and Anglo-French Cemetery, 18th Division Memorial; The Ulster Tower Visitor Centre and Memorials; Beaumont Hamel Newfoundland Visitor Centre, Memorial Park, preserved trenches, Memorials and CWGC Cemeteries; Serre – CWGC Cemeteries Nos 2 and 1, French Cemetery and Chapel, 12th Bn York & Lancs Memorial.

• **Extra Visits:** Rancourt Souvenir Français Chapel, British, French & German Cemeteries; Foch Statue, Bouchavesnes; Australian 2nd Division Memorial, Mont St Quentin; The Historial Museum, Péronne; Serre Road No 3, Queen's and Railway Hollow CWGC Cemeteries, Sheffield Memorial Park and its 'Pals' Memorials.

• **Planned duration, without stops for refreshments or extra visits:** 8 hours
• **Total distance:** 26.5 miles
• **Distance from Calais to start point via A26 to Arras and A1 to Bapaume and D929 to Albert:** 100 miles. Motorway Tolls
• **Base Towns:** Arras, Albert, Amiens
• **Maps:** Major & Mrs Holt's Battle Map of the Somme; Michelin 286 France Nord Flandres - Artois – Picardie: 1:200,000

From Calais take the A16/A26 direction Paris/Reims then the A26 direction St Omer. Continue to the motorway junction with the A1 beyond Arras Centre and take the A1 signed Paris/Arras-Est to Exit 14, Bapaume. At the roundabout follow signs to Albert on the ring road and then on the D929 via Warlencourt and le Sars. You will then pass several sites of interest that will be visited later in the tour. Enter Albert and turn right following signs to Amiens and drive down the rue Birmingham towards the Basilique which is surmounted by a golden figure holding aloft a baby. If possible stop in the parking area in the square. Set your mileometer to zero.

• ALBERT/GOLDEN MADONNA/SOMME '14-'18 MUSEUM/MAC CARTON MURAL/0 MILES/45 MINUTES/RWC/MAP 5/1

Fierce fighting around Albert began in the early months of the war, the first enemy shelling being on 29 September 1914. By October 1916, when the Somme

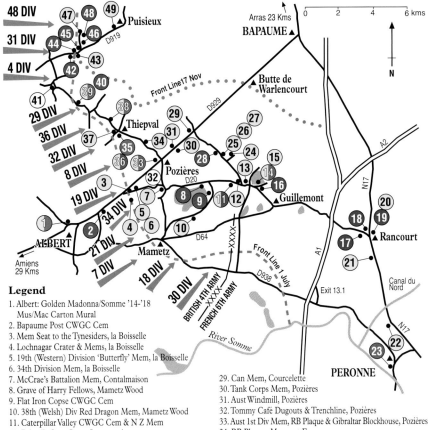

Golden Madonna on the steeple to an angle below horizontal, but it did not fall. Visible to soldiers of both sides for many miles around, the statue gave rise to two legends. The British and French believed that the war would end on the day that the statue fell (it is said that the Allied Staff sent engineers up the steeple at night to shore it up to prevent raising false hopes). The Germans believed that whoever knocked down the Madonna would lose the war. Neither prediction came to pass. During the German occupation from March to August 1918 the British shelled Albert and knocked down the Golden Virgin. The figure was never found and today's statue is a replica. The townspeople strongly resisted the suggestion to remount it in its wartime leaning position. The Basilique was rebuilt to the original design by the son of the original architect, Duthoit, with sculptures by Albert Roze. Most of the town (notably the station) was rebuilt in the 1920s in the distinct Art Deco style then in vogue. The idea to declare it a Zone Rouge (too dangerous to rebuild, like some of the battlefields around Verdun) was also strongly resisted by the inhabitants of Albert.

To the right of the church is the entrance to

SOMME '14-'18 TRENCH MUSEUM

This interesting and well-presented museum has been made in the subterranean tunnels under the Basilique and other parts of the town. To either side of the main corridor are realistic scenes and sound effects of 1914-18 trench and dugout life – British, French and German – with informative captions in all three languages translated by Paula Flanagan Kesteloot. They are full of authentic artefacts and weapons. Visitors emerge through a souvenir/book shop into the pleasant arboretum public gardens.

Legend

1. Albert: Golden Madonna/Somme '14-'18 Mus/Mac Carton Mural
2. Bapaume Post CWGC Cem
3. Mem Seat to the Tynesiders, la Boisselle
4. Lochnagar Crater & Mems, la Boisselle
5. 19th (Western) Division 'Butterfly' Mem, la Boisselle
6. 34th Division Mem, la Boisselle
7. McCrae's Battalion Mem, Contalmaison
8. Grave of Harry Fellows, Mametz Wood
9. Flat Iron Copse CWGC Cem
10. 38th (Welsh) Div Red Dragon Mem, Mametz Wood
11. Caterpillar Valley CWGC Cem & N Z Mem
12. Bristol's Own Cross, Longueval
13. Pipers' Mem, Longueval
14. S. African Nat Mem, & Mus, Delville Wood
15. Mems to Welsh VCs & Original Hornbeam, Delville Wood
16. Delville Wood CWGC Cem
17. Ger Cem, Rancourt
18. Rancourt Mil CWGC Cem
19. Fr Nat Cem, Rancourt
20. *Souvenir Français* Chapel, Rancourt
21. Statue of Marshal Foch, Bouchavesnes-Bergen
22. Aust 2nd Div Mem, Mont St Quentin
23. Historial Mus, Péronne
24. Cameron Highlanders & Black Watch Mem, High Wood
25. 47th (London) Div Mem, High Wood
26. 20th Bn RF Mem Tree, High Wood
27. Glasgow Highlanders' Cairn, High Wood
28. London CWGC Cem + Ext, High Wood
29. Can Mem, Courcelette
30. Tank Corps Mem, Pozières
31. Aust Windmill, Pozières
32. Tommy Café Dugouts & Trenchline, Pozières
33. Aust 1st Div Mem, RB Plaque & Gibraltar Blockhouse, Pozières
34. RB Plaque, Mouquet Farm
35. Thiepval Visitor & Information Centre
36. Thiepval Mem to the Missing/CWGC & Fr Cems
37. 18th Div Mem, Thiepval
38. Ulster Tower, Mems & Visitor Centre
39. Newfoundland Mem Park, Visitor Centre, Mems & Preserved Trenches
40. CWGC Cems, Newfoundland Mem Park
41. 'Ocean Villas' Café Trenchline & WW1 Cellar
42. Serre Road CWGC Cem No 2
43. Fr Mem Chapel, Serre
44. Fr Nat Cem, Serre
45. Serre Road CWGC Cem No 1
46. Serre Road CWGC Cem No 3
47. Sheffield Mem Park & Mems
48. Railway Hollow, Queen's & Luke Copse CWGC Cems
49. 12th Bn York & Lancs Mem, Serre

© TVH 2005

THE SOMME: 1 JULY 1916

offensive had pushed the German guns out of range, the town was a pile of red rubble. On 26 March 1918, during their final offensive, Albert was taken by the Germans and retaken by the British on 22 August, the East Surreys entering the town at bayonet point. Albert was a major administration and control centre for the Somme offensive, and it was from here that the first Press message was sent announcing the start of the 'Big Push'.

The golden figure above you is the Virgin Mary holding aloft the baby Jesus. It stands on top of the Basilique of Notre-Dame des Brébières. Before the war thousands of pilgrims came annually to see the black Madonna inside the church which, legend says, had been discovered locally by a shepherd in the Middle Ages (hence the church's name, from brébis, the word for ewe). In January 1915 German shelling toppled the

OPEN:
every day 1 February-15 December 0930-1200 and 1400-1800. June-September 0930-1800.
Entrance fee payable.
Tel: + (0)3 22 75 16 17.
Fax: + (0)3 22 75 56 33.
E-mail: **musee.des.abris.somme.1916@wanadoo.fr**
Website: **www.musee-somme-1916.org/**
www.somme-trench-museum.co.uk

On the wall opposite the top exit to the park is a striking Mural by Albert Mac Carton showing the Basilique with the Madonna, leaning perilously, and the figures of Allied soldiers. In the small garden in front of it is a Plaque to commemorate the inauguration of the mural on 29 June 1996.

Return up rue Birmingham and turn left on the D929 signed A1/Lille/Bapaume.

You are now moving along the axis of the British attack of 1 July 1916.

Continue to the second large roundabout.

On top of the roundabout a controversial 4-metre high statue of a British Tommy clambering out of his trench holding his rifle is planned for 2005. Made of resin and painted in lifelike colours he charges towards the German lines. The statue was the initiative of the Albert Museum and is funded by the Museum, the town of Albert and the Somme Conseil Général. The Conseil is among sponsors (including Lions, Rotary, Airbus and Crédit Mutuel) for a Poppy Country Marathon, to be run on 3 July 2005 starting from Albert, to raise money for charity. It was the brainchild of Paul Chaplin, a British teacher living on the Somme. For details see **www.somme-marathon.com**

Continue following Bapaume signs to the cemetery on the right.

Entrance to the Somme '14-'18 Museum.

Maquette of the proposed Tommy Statue, Albert.

• BAPAUME POST CWGC CEMETERY/1.3 MILES/10 MINUTES/MAP 5/2

One of the first cemeteries in this sector to be completed, it contains two battalion commanders of the Tyneside Brigade: Lt Cols William Lyle and Charles Sillery, lying side by side in Row IG, both killed on 1 July.

Continue up and then down over the hill (known as the Tara-Usna line), passing the Poppy Restaurant on the right, to the junction in la Boisselle.

This was the British front line and here there is a Memorial Seat to the Tynesiders (Map 5/3). (Those who are fortunate enough to possess a copy of John Masefield's classic The Old Front Line will find many of its descriptions still valid from this point onwards.)

Fork right on the D20 before the seat and turn first right following signs to la Grande Mine on the C9.

• LOCHNAGAR CRATER & MEMORIALS, LA BOISSELLE/2.7 MILES/20 MINUTES/ MAP 5/4

The land containing the crater was purchased in 1978 and is maintained privately by Englishman Richard Dunning as a personal memorial to all those who fought in the Battle of the Somme and in particular to those, of both

sides, killed in the crater. Other memorials have subsequently been erected there: a Stone in Memory of Pte Tom Easton of the 2nd Bn Tyneside Scottish; a Memorial Seat 'Donated by friends who visit in memory of friends who remain'; Memorial Seats to veteran Harry Fellows and to the Grimsby Chums; a wooden Cross in memory of Pte George Nugent whose remains were found on the spot on 31 October 1998 and a Plaque to Gnr W.G. Noon. At the entrance is a CGS/H Information Panel.

Golden Madonna and Murel, Albert.

Diorama, Somme '14-'18 Museum.

Cairn to McCrae's Bn, Contalmaison.

Tynesiders Memorial seat, la Boisselle.

First of July Ceremony Lochnager Crater.

Richard, who is intensely aware of the historical and spiritual value of the crater, of its ability to shock and evoke the violence of war through its sheer size, has also raised a simple 12ft high Cross made from church timber originating on Tyneside. Much work has recently been undertaken to enhance the feeling that one is entering a very Special Memorial area and a 'living' Garden of Remembrance. One passes through large stone curbs and 'knife-rests' along duckboards and a hedge bounds the site.

Richard may be contacted on 01483 810651. On 1 July each year at 0728 a simple but very moving and involving memorial gathering takes place at the crater. There is also a ceremony here on 11 November. All members of the public are able to attend either ceremony. **N.B. It is forbidden to climb down into the crater because of the damage it causes to this fast-eroding precious remnant of the war.**

Mine warfare had been carried on in this area well before July 1916 and there were many craters in No Man's Land. In June, along the Western Front as a whole, the British had blown 101 mines and the Germans 126. In this area some of the shafts dug, from which tunnels then reached out to the enemy line, were over 100ft deep with tunnels at up to four levels.

Below left; German trumpeter at the ceremony.

Below right; First of July Ceremony Lochnagar Crater.

When dug, the mine here was known as Lochnagar, and had been started by 185th Tunnelling Company in December 1915. It was finished by 179th Tunnelling Company and packed with two charges of 24,000 and 36,000 lb of ammonal. Seventeen British mines, including Lochnagar, were exploded at 0728 hours along the front on 1 July and the circular crater here measured 300ft across and was 90ft deep. Debris rose 4,000ft into the air and, as it settled the attack began. It failed. The attacking battalions of Tyneside Scottish followed by the Tyneside Irish were reduced to small parties of survivors.

Following the failure of the attack by the Tynesiders of 34th Division, the 10th Worcesters were ordered to move up from beside Albert to make an assault at dawn on 2 July. So chaotic were conditions in the communication trenches that the battalion got lost, and the attack did not go in until 3 July. The Worcesters took the crater area and the village, Pte F.G. Turrall winning a VC in the process, but the battalion lost a third of its fighting strength and the Commanding Officer was killed.

Return to the village and turn right on the D20. Continue to the church on the left.

It was in la Boisselle on 2-3 July that the extraordinary Belgian-born officer, T/Lt Col Adrian Carton de Wiart, commanding the 8th Gloucesters, won his VC for forcing home the attack and controlling the commands of three other battalion commanders who had been wounded while exposing himself fearlessly to the enemy. He was wounded eight times during WW1 (including the loss of an eye and his left hand) went on to become Lt Gen Sir Adrian Carton de Wiart, KBE, CB, CMG, DSO, with many foreign awards and distinguished service that took him to Poland, Norway, Yugoslavia, Italy and China in WW2.

In front of the church is:

19TH (WESTERN) DIVISION 'BUTTERFLY' MEMORIAL/3.2 MILES/5 MINUTES/ MAP 5/5

This Memorial, with its butterfly emblem carved on the top, commemorates their casualties of 2 July-20 November at la Boisselle, Bazentin le Petit and Grandcourt. The Divisional Units are inscribed on the base. The Division took the village on 4 July 1916.

Continue to the end of the houses on the left. Up a track to the left is:

34TH DIVISION MEMORIAL/3.3 MILES/10 MINUTES/MAP 5/6

The figure of Victory (minus her original laurel wreath) commemorates the Division's exploits here on 1 July 1916. It incorporates their distinctive checkerboard emblem and the composition of the Divisional Units. Beyond the memorial the top of the Thiepval Memorial and Ovillers CWGC Cemetery may be seen.

Continue to Contalmaison, passing a sign to Gordon Dump CWGC Cemetery on the right. In the village, after passing a sign to Contalmaison Château CWGC Cemetery to the left, turn right on the D147 and stop by the church.

MEMORIAL TO McCRAE'S BATTALION, CONTALMAISON/4.9 MILES/5 MINUTES/ MAP 5/7

Dedicated on 7 November 2004 this 10ft high cairn of Elgin stone commemorates the remarkable Battalion of Lt Col Sir George McCrae, the 16th Royal Scots, who on 1 July 1916 captured the German strong point known as Scots Redoubt in the ruins of Contalmaison. Their story is told on superb bronze relief plaques on the cairn showing the 34th Division's chequerboard insignia, a cartoon that was the regimental Christmas card for 1916, the figure of Sir George, the Heart of Midlothian Football Club's sacrifice and details of the unveiling and local cooperation. The full story of Sir George and his brave battalion and Jack Alexander's efforts to resurrect 1920 memorial plans was told in the Spring 2004 edition of The New Chequers, the Journal of the 'Friends of Lochnagar'.

Return to the junction and turn right following signs to Bazentin and Longueval on the D20, skirting Mametz Wood on the right.

'The British keep
charging forward.
Despite the fact
that hundreds are
already lying dead
in the shell holes to
our front, fresh
waves keep
emerging from the
assault trenches
over there.
We have got to
fire!'

THE GERMAN ARMY ON THE SOMME - 1ST JULY 1916

Dawn broke on a perfect summer's day on 1st July. Allied artillery and mortar fire rained down at an unprecedented rate, even by the standards of the past week. The nervous tension in the dugouts of the waiting German defenders was almost tangible. They knew beyond doubt that the long-awaited offensive was about to begin.

By Jack Sheldon

This article was extracted from Jack Sheldon's book, *The German Army on the Somme 1914 - 1916* and is reproduced here by permission of Pen and Sword Books Ltd.

They knew too that they had one chance and one chance only when the barrage lifted: if they wanted to live, they had to win the race to their parapet. If they were out of their dugouts, complete with their weapons and spare ammunition, before the attackers arrived, they would probably prevail. Caught underground, death or capture was their inevitable fate. They fastened on their equipment and checked and rechecked their weapons. All along the line, from Gommecourt to Chaulnes, sentries crouching in the entrances to their dugouts strained to detect a slackening in the fire, then suddenly, at 8.20 a.m. German time, the artillery fire lifted and there was an almighty roar, as a gigantic charge exploded beneath the men of 9th Company Reserve Infantry Regiment 119 who were manning trenches on

Heavily armed German troops on the Somme with captured British Lewis guns, some of them equipped with thick shoulder straps for pulling heavy machine guns up to the front line.

Hawthorn Ridge overlooking Beaumont Hamel. The After Action Report of 3rd Battalion Reserve Infantry Regiment 1191 1. noted:

> At 8.15 am [this is an error, 8.20 am German time, 7.20 British time], a mine with an extraordinarily large charge was blown under the projecting 'nose' in the middle of B1. Almost all of 1st Platoon (Leutnant Renz) and elements on the left of the 2nd Platoon (Leutnant Böhm) were crushed and buried in their dugouts by the explosion. All the entrances to the 3rd Platoon dugouts (Leutnant Breitmeyer) and some of those belonging to the dugouts of the 2nd Platoon (Leutnant Böhm) were buried by falling rock. Only very few men of the 9th Company, those on the left flank and the right flank where the machine guns were located, succeeded in get-

A comfortable German dugout during a quiet spell in the fighting. Note the heavy machine-gun in place between sand bags.

The awful result of a direct artillery hit on a German dugout.

ting straight out into the open and occupying their battle positions. The enormous crater was about fifty metres long and fifteen metres deep. Within a few moments further men managed to dig themselves out, so that the 9th Company had about two sections ready to do battle.

All around, the layer of white chalk gave the impression that there had been a snowstorm. Flares calling for artillery defensive fire shot upwards.

The defenders were beginning to react, but not before some British troops had stormed into the trenches of 3rd Platoon to the left of the crater. Inside one of the dugouts, which had four entrances, three of which were blocked and only a small hole remained of the fourth, the occupants, who included Leutnant Breitmeyer and the company commander, Reserve *Oberleutnant* Mühlbayer, worked feverishly to escape. Before the sentry could enlarge the hole fully, he was bayoneted and fell back dead down the stairs. Standing by him, Vizefeldwebel Davidsohn shot his assailant in the face with a flare. Hand grenades and smoke bombs were thrown into the dugout and demands for its surrender were shouted down. The defenders, in hope and expectation of reinforcement and support from elsewhere, did not deign to reply and soon a pitched battle for possession of the crater and its surroundings was in full flow.

Further north, at Gommecourt, the barrage lifted a few minutes later. There was absolutely no surprise here. Not only did the defenders know that the attack was coming, they also had a clear idea about its aims, as a result of intelligence gleaned a few days previously from the interrogation of the captured Private Wheat, who was a member of 5th Battalion North Staffordshire Regiment of the 46th (North Midland) Division. The

> 'The weapon commander, Gefreiter Füchte, noticed... two forms suddenly in a thick cloud of gas. He jumped onto the shot-up parapet and killed a British officer, before being killed himself by a hand grenade.'

German defences north of the village in the area of Reserve Infantry Regiment 91 had been considerably weakened by the bombardment. The barbed wire obstacle was badly damaged and the trenches were blown in and flattened. However, almost all of the dugouts and hence the soldiers had survived the bombardment. Here the assault succeeded in breaking into the forward trenches, but vigorous local counter-attacks swiftly restored the situation. South of the village the main weight of the attack fell on Sectors G5, N1 and N2, [the three sectors immediately south and south-east of the village] which were defended by Infantry Regiment 170. The British troops from the 56th (London) Division succeeded in breaching the defences, which led to hard, confused fighting and a violent reaction from the defenders. Infantry Regiment 170 appealed to Reserve Infantry Regiment 55 for assistance, reporting;

Enemy attack in Target Areas 16/18 at 08.35 am; gas attack against Sector North at 9.05; attack at 9.15 am against Sector 19. At 9.30 the enemy broke into G5 and is threatening the right flank. We are holding the third trench.'4

At 9.30 am a Regimental order was given to 3rd Battalion Reserve Infantry Regiment 55: 'Major Tauscher and his Battalion, including the Construction Company, are to attack, via the 2nd Guards position, the enemy which has broken into G5 and drive them out. Report when ready. Machine guns will be made available. The battalion commander is to be on Hill 147.'

Help was on the way. The ensuing battle, which involved hand to hand fighting, lasted until the late afternoon, but finally the defenders prevailed; the attackers being killed or driven out. It was a hard but successful day and especially so for the machine-gun crews, which had been deployed in a reinforcing role in G5 just south of the village.

Leutnant Koch Machine Gun Scharfschützen-Trupp 736.

It should also be noted that the two gunners of Machine Gun 8, who were still unhurt after the weapon had been overrun in the first rush, immediately and without being prevented by the British, dragged the gun into a dugout, covered it with a groundsheet and sat on it. So they were able later, at a suitable moment, to bring the gun into action against the withdrawing enemy. The weapon commander, Gefreiter Füchte, noticed... two forms suddenly in a thick cloud of gas. [This must have been smoke or dust. The only release of cylinder gas anywhere on the British sector that day was at Fricourt.] *He jumped onto the shot-up parapet and killed a British officer, before being killed himself by a hand grenade. His courageous behaviour made it possible for the gunners to bring the weapon into action. Unteroffizier Schultheiss got his gun into action in G5 in good time and caused heavy casualties to the enemy. Gefreiter Freiburger acted as Gunner 3. Gunners Haupt, Meyer, Hast and Gefreiter Berkefeld attended to ammunition resupply. Suddenly the enemy appeared in their rear and threw hand grenades. Freiberger was severely wounded; Haupt, Meyer and Hast were wounded too. The British called upon Unteroffizier Schultheiss to surrender. Schultheiss, who was being resupplied with ammunition by Berkefeld, refused. He swung his gun round and fired to the rear until both men, who were attacked from all sides with hand grenades, were killed. Weapon 7 was located to the right of Weapon 6 and was commanded by Gefreiter Niemeyer. Niemeyer succeeded in beating off the enemy, both those to his front as well as those who had broken into the trench to one side and his rear. He caused the enemy many casualties and prevented enemy exploitation to the right. When Niemeyer was killed by a shot to the head, Hennig continued to operate the gun with great success against the fleeing masses of British. Examination of the corpses showed that he had fired with great calmness and excellent dispersion of fire.'*

Altogether during the fight for Gommecourt, Reserve Infantry Regiments 55 and 91 lost three officers and 182 men, but lying before the position of Reserve Infantry Regiment 91 were 700 dead British soldiers and as many as 2,000 in front of Reserve Infantry Regiment 55.7 A

> '*He swung his gun round and fired to the rear until both men, who were attacked from all sides with hand grenades, were killed.*'

little further to the south, a major disaster for the British army was unfolding to the west of the village of Serre where, it will be remembered, there had been a hard-fought battle the previous year. Here the defenders had learned and applied critical lessons. They were now occupying the vital high ground around Serre. It was critical to the integrity of the entire defence north of the Ancre that this place did not fall, so the German army had spent over a year turning it into a virtually impregnable fortress. Promptly at 8.30 a.m., the Pals Battalions of the 31st Division went over the top into a maelstrom of fire. Incredible to relate, thanks to fortuitous selection of a partially covered approach route, a handful of them actually penetrated as far as Serre village itself, but none lived to tell the tale. The attack was simply ripped to shreds by the men of Infantry Regiment 169 from Baden, ably assisted by machine gunners from Infantry Regiment 66, which was located slightly to the north.

Unteroffizier Otto Lais Infantry Regiment 1698.

'*Wild firing slammed into the masses of the enemy. All around us was the rushing, whistling and roaring of a storm; a hurricane, as the destructive British shells rushed towards our artillery which was firing courageously, our reserves and our rear areas. Throughout all this racket, this rumbling, growling, bursting, cracking and wild banging and crashing of small arms, could be heard the heavy, hard and regular Tack! Tack! of the machine guns... That one firing slower, this other with a faster rhythm – it was the precision work of fine material and skill – and both were playing a gruesome tune to the enemy, whilst providing their own comrades and the men manning the automatic rifles a high degree of security and reassurance.*

A machine-gun captain surveys No Man's Land for targets which were plentiful on 1st July. Machine guns overheated quickly due to the constant rate of fire, causing the operators to suffer burns and swelling to the hands.

British troops advancing stealthily towards the German lines under heavy fire. Many of their comrades would have already been cut down in their thousands.

The machine gunners, who lived a privileged life at quiet times and were envied for being able to avoid jobs such as carrying heavy mortar rounds forward, were earning their pay today. Belt after belt was fired. 250 rounds – 1,000 – 3,000. Pass up the spare barrels! shouts the gun commander. Barrels are changed – fire on! 5,000 rounds. The barrel must be changed again. It's red hot and the cooling water is boiling – the hands working the weapon are scorched and burned – 'Keep firing!' urges the gun commander, 'or shoot yourself!' The cooling water turns to seething steam with the continuous firing. In the heat of battle, the steam overflow pipe slips out of its fixing on the water jacket. With a great hiss, a jet of steam goes up, providing a superb target for the enemy. It is the greatest good fortune that they have the sun in their eyes and we have it at our backs. The enemy closes up nearer. We fire on endlessly. There is less steam. A further barrel change is urgent. The cooling water has almost steamed away. 'Where's the water?' bawls the gunner. 'Get the mineral water out of the dugout!' 'There's none left Unteroffizier!' It all went during the eight day bombardment.

The British keep charging forward. Despite the fact that hundreds are already lying dead in the shell holes to our front, fresh waves keep emerging from the assault trenches over there. We have got to fire! A gunner rushes into the crater with the water container and urinates into it. A second pisses into it too – quick, refill! The British have closed to grenade throwing range

> Keep firing! urges the gun commander, 'or shoot yourself!' The cooling water turns to seething steam with the continuous firing.

and hand grenades fly backwards and forwards. The barrel change is complete, the water jacket refilled. Load! Hand and rifle grenades burst close to the weapon. Just keep calm, get the tangle sorted out and load! Speak loudly, slowly and clearly to yourself. Forward! – Down! – Back! (Working parts forward – Belt on – Working parts back). The same again! – Safety catch to the right! – Fire!'...Tack! – Tack! Tack! – Tack!...Once more rapid fire slams into the clay pit to our front. High pillars of steam rise from all the machine guns. Most of the steam hoses have been torn off or shot away. Skin hangs in ribbons from the fingers of the burnt hands of the gunners and gun commanders! Constant pressure by their left thumbs on the triggers has turned them into swollen, shapeless lumps of flesh. Their hands rest, as though cramped, on the vibrating weapons.

18,000 rounds! The other platoon weapon has a stoppage. Gunner Schwarz falls shot through the head, over the belt he is feeding. The belt twists, feeds rounds into the gun crookedly and they jam! Next man forward! The dead man is removed. The gunner strips the feed mechanism, removes the rounds and reloads. Fire; pause; barrel change; fetch ammunition; lay the dead and wounded on the floor of the crater. That is the hard, unrelenting tempo of the morning of 1st July 1916. The sound of machine gun fire can be heard right across the divisional front. The youth of England, the finest regiments of Scotland [Lais is mistaken. No Scottish regiments attacked Serre that day] bled to death in front of Serre. The weapon which was commanded by Unteroffizier Koch from Pforzheim and which was stationed directly on the Serre-Mailly road fires off a last belt! It has fired no fewer 20,000 rounds at the British!

South of Serre, on the slopes of Redan Ridge below Soden Redoubt, the men of Reserve Infantry Regiment 121 had prepared an unpleasant surprise for any would-be attacker. The Heidenkopf [Quadrilateral], which jutted forward from the German front line had been prepared as a massive booby trap for attacking infantry. It came under heavy artillery fire during the bombardment, was completely evacuated on 28th June, but was reoccupied by a skeleton group of defenders in time for 1st July. There was a realization that this area could not be held in the short term in the event of a major attack. So the idea developed to lure a large number of attackers into it and to blow them up by means of hidden mines. In the event the plan was much less successful than intended, because the Heidenkopf was not attacked directly. Instead the main British attack swept around it and in fact at least one of the charges may have been set off prematurely, blowing up or burying some of the defenders. Finally the mines were blown, but they achieved comparatively little, except to be the subject of a detailed report by the German engineers later:

A German mine exploding in No Man's Land. The debris thrown up by such an explosion was equally as deadly as the blast.

[At 8.25 a.m.] *it was noted that ...strong British forces were massing around the Heidenkopf* [Quadrilateral] *and that they suddenly paused in their forward movement. There was no trace of the later fate of the guards of the Heidenkopf and mined dugout. After recapture only the Officer in charge was found and he was lying dead in Bayerngraben* [Bavarian Trench]... *During the nights which followed the attack, engineer patrols established the extent of the explosion. There were great surface changes. Four large craters surrounded the flattened Quadrilateral Trench. Detonation in all four of the chambers was successful. The weight of the charges was: Ia = 1500kg; Ib = 1500kg; IIa = 1500kg; IIb = 1250kg.*

For the three craters on the right, the dimensions were the same. They measured twenty-five metres in diameter and ten to fifteen metres in depth. The left hand crater was somewhat smaller. The extent to which casualties were caused could be established from the many British dead who were killed by falling rock. The British troops seem to have been especially surprised by the two left hand craters. Our underground installations are still more or less in order. The communication dug out (Stollen II) [Mined dugout II] *is already useable once more from Bavarian Trench to the Heidenkopf. For the time being, it is being used as an access route to a forward double sentry post which has been established at the staircase entrance in the old Heidenkopf.*

The British did not actually attack the Heidenkopf. They pushed on left and right of it to Bavarian Trench. As was later established, none of the British remained in the Heidenkopf itself; this despite the fact that they established themselves temporarily behind it in Bavarian Trench. It was only in consequence of the lack of

'No doubt the British had suspected the presence of hidden mines in the Heidenkopf. They attempted, therefore, to bypass it to the sides and to enter it from the rear.'

clarity and the confusion caused in the massed British ranks by the German fire that they closed in on the area of the Heidenkopf. Nevertheless, the explosion, which took place ten to fifteen minutes after the first British line had broken in, caused casualties. No doubt the British had suspected the presence of hidden mines in the Heidenkopf. They attempted, therefore, to bypass it to the sides and to enter it from the rear. What led the British to this assumption is impossible to say. Possibly it was the conclusion they drew from the shape of the Heidenkopf. The section of trench which sticks out well forward of the main line could have suggested that it would be cleared during an attack and be used as a trap for the advancing enemy. It is almost impossible to believe that they had exact knowledge of the location of the hidden mines. This particular case underlines the fact that hidden mines should not be laid in obvious parts of the position. As soon as the enemy develops a suspicion he can divert around the feared place.*

This was the reason why he by-passed the open Beaumont North minefield, attacking only to the left and right of it. Hidden mines have proved themselves to be technically hard to employ. If they are laid sufficiently powerful to be effective, their explosion is inconsistent with the most reliable trench defence. In view of the resultant rock fall, nearby trenches can only be occupied after a successful explosion. It is really extremely difficult to judge the correct moment

83

for the explosion. In the current case, observers could not do their work reliably, despite all the preparations. News concerning the British advance reached the firing point only in a roundabout way. Strictly speaking the explosion occurred far too late. The Heidenkopf experience demonstrates that it is not worth placing hidden charges in developed minefields. The simplest and most effective way to use these minefields is to bring them into use as accommodation for the reinforced trench garrison. They perform outstanding service as stores for hand grenades, matériel and rations. The blowing of individual positions is to be condemned...

Elsewhere, throughout most of the length of Redan Ridge, the attackers were beaten back, mown down by interlocking machine-gun fire from depth positions and the flanks, without ever penetrating the German positions. Here and there minor incursions were achieved, but within an hour of the start of the attack, the entire position, less the Heidenkopf, was back in the hands of Reserve Infantry Regiment 121. During the course of the morning it was decided to recapture the Heidenkopf too. Reinforcements arrived from the 3rd Battalion Reserve Infantry Regiment 121 and a platoon, commanded by Leutnant Hoppe, came over from the neighbouring Infantry Regiment 169 to help. The clearance operation began and step by step the British troops were forced back out. It was a slow process. Casualties were heavy on both sides, because the British built and manned a series of barricades, defended by Lewis gun teams and yielded ground only slowly. Late in the day, as it began to go dark, there was only one small pocket of resistance left. This, too, was attacked and eliminated. Those British soldiers, who did not escape back to their original lines, were captured. Only relatively few prisoners were taken on 1st July, but a systematic search of the recaptured area and the cratered zone in front of the position the following day yielded many more. In the end 200 men were sent to the rear.

The Heidenkopf itself was a shambles. There were corpses everywhere, both British and German, some of them heaped high. Smashed and abandoned equipment lay all around in a scene of total devastation. This small area alone claimed the lives of about 150 men of Reserve Infantry Regiment 121 and nearly 500 British soldiers, but there were also 1,200 dead piled up in front of the 1st Battalion and 576 in front of the 2nd Battalion. The German defenders were struck by the quality of men who attacked them and how well they were equipped; remarking, in particular, on the fact that each carried

> There were corpses everywhere, both British and German, some of them heaped high.

washing and shaving equipment and that those taken prisoner had no sooner been taken into a dugout than they began to shave! Back at the area south of the Beaumont Hamel – Auchonvillers road, the scene in and around Hawthorn Crater was one of complete bloody carnage. The men of the mauled 9th Company of Reserve Infantry Regiment 119 were able to play little part in the fighting, but adjoining companies wrought enormous execution in the ranks of the attackers. For a while, the situation around the newly blown crater was extremely tense, but reserves began to arrive in short order, as platoons of the 7th and 12th Companies, accompanied by two 'musketen' [automatic rifles], raced forward from the third trench to the threatened place and occupied a rough firing line in shell holes overlooking the road. The attack was in any case withering away, thanks to rapid fire from machine guns of Reserve Infantry Regiment 121 located in the so-called 'Bergwerk' [Mine] behind Beaumont village. There followed a short period of close quarter fighting. A British aircraft flew over and dropped bombs on the reinforcements from the 12th Company, without achieving much, an increasing number of trapped soldiers from the 9th Company managed to dig themselves free and gradually the situation here on the right flank of Reserve Infantry Regiment 119 swung completely in favour of the defenders.

500 metres to the south, the defenders of the Leilingschlucht [Y Ravine] sector could not have been better placed to repel the heavy attacks which were about to be launched. The roar of the mine blowing up provided them with the best possible warning. They then benefited greatly from the extraordinary error made by the British VIII Corps in that arrangements had been

A youthful German soldier killed in the fighting on 1st July 1916.

made to lift almost all the suppressive fire from 0820. As a result, the garrison which, thanks to the geography of the area barely suffered at all during the bombardment, was able to take up its firing positions in a completely calm and methodical manner. Here there was no need for them to win a race to the parapet. They and all the other troops manning the positions down to the Ancre Valley had been given a generous start. Their barbed wire obstacle was largely intact. The machine guns were set up carefully and riflemen adopted optimum fire positions. Extra ammunition was carried up and prepared, then section and platoon commanders issued final orders. The commanding officer of 3rd Battalion Reserve Infantry Regiment 119 later reported;

> The enemy attacked all along the line in great strength. The entire garrison was able to occupy battle positions and then to open fire. The telephone link to the artillery was destroyed, so it was not possible to call for defensive fire by this means. The sector command staff and the companies fired red flares into the air, but when it came the defensive fire was weak and far from comprehensive.

In the circumstances, it was just as well for the defenders that this area was covered with a very large number of well placed machine guns. Quite apart from those located in and around the first position, a line of eight weapons spaced out in depth and occupying concealed, mined out positions just to the north of Station Road, which ran from Beaumont village to Beaumont station, wreaked havoc. It is extremely doubtful if the attackers located any of these weapons, or were even aware that they were being engaged by them. Within minutes of the start of the attack, the survivors were pinned down in shell holes in front of the German First Position.

The Battle Log of the 3rd Battalion Reserve Infantry Regiment 119 describes, in a few terse entries, the methodical destruction of the first wave of attackers from the British 29th Division. Because the timing of the blowing of the mine is given as 8.15 a.m., it is possible that the remainder of the timings are also five minutes ahead of the actual timings involved:

8.15 a.m: Mine blown in B1.

8.20 a.m: B1-B3 under attack.

8.30 a.m: The British are lying down 100 metres short of the first trench of B3. Own machine guns have opened fire.

8.35 a.m: B2 reports: Attack stalled. Masses of British soldiers are lying in the hollow in front of Target Area 46. Machine guns are being moved forward from the second to the first trench.

8.40 a.m: B2 reports: The British are lying in front of the first trench and are being shot to pieces. No defensive fire is coming down in the hollow in front of Target Area 46; a battalion is gathering there to launch an attack.

Sector Order: Destroy them with machine-gun fire…'

As the morning wore on, any minor incursions into the line had all been mopped up. The well-known tragedy of the destruction of 1st Battalion Essex Regiment and 1st Battalion Newfoundland Regiment just to the south of Y Ravine had come and gone, without any detectable difference in tone in the German battle log. Early problems with defensive fire had been largely resolved. It was soon coming down where it was needed and the defending infantry had had the situation under control from very early on in the attack. If attackers appeared to their front they simply shot them to a standstill. By 2.00 p.m. calm prevailed all along the regimental front, which was covered from end to end by the dead and dying attackers. Their own casualties for the period since the start of the bombardment were only seven officers and 144 men killed, twenty-four of whom were buried alive; six officers and 266 other ranks were wounded.

Reserve Infantry Regiment 99, which had the task of defending the strategically vital Thiepval Ridge, had a much harder, more trying, time of it. Here the stakes could not have been higher. Both sides were well aware of that fact and initially the British obtained an advantage. Men of the 36th Ulster Division charged with capturing the vital Schwaben Redoubt and pressing on towards Grandcourt, behaved very boldly. No Man's Land was quite narrow to the north of Thiepval village, the neutralizing barrage, fired partly by first class French batteries, was effective up to the last minute and the first wave of the assaulting force made good use of the cover it provided, by crawling forward to within forty – fifty metres of the German front line before the attack proper was due to begin. As a result, here the attackers won the race to the parapet.

> The enemy attack on C2 and C3 was conducted with such aggression that the two machine guns could only fire for a short time before they were both overrun. More than half of both teams were killed or wounded by artillery fire. The remaining weapons in C1, C4 and the Strassburger Steige [Strasbourg Slope] were operated with outstanding effect. Despite some stoppages, which were merely attributed to the ammunition, they fired almost ceaselessly. The Russian machine gun in the Schwaben Redoubt did not come into action, because a direct hit shortly before the assault buried the gun and three quarters of its crew. Both the Platoon Commander and his runner, who hurried to the spot to dig them out, were killed by shrapnel. The Fasbender platoon in Schwaben Redoubt was ordered to occupy the front line position in the Redoubt. During the attack the German weapons on the left flank of C3 and the right of C4 were put out of action by direct hits. The crews moved to the intact German weapons and also manned a captured British machine gun, with which they immediately opened fire on the advancing British soldiers.

The breakthrough point had been selected skilfully, because the southern part of C3 was largely in dead ground from C4. This also favoured the further advance to Schwaben Redoubt. In sub-sectors C2 and C3, every man not killed or wounded was captured, but such was the generally confused nature of the fighting that some of the prisoners escaped. According to Oberstleutnant Bram, Commander of Bavarian Reserve Infantry Regiment 8, Reserve Leutnant Schmidt of 7th Company Reserve Infantry Regiment 99, who was deployed in C4, reported that:

a number of Bavarians arrived in his location. No sooner had they been captured, than they had escaped. The British had already taken their watches, money and rings. Once they had been equipped with weapons taken from the wounded, they played a full part in the fighting.

Hauptmann Schorer, Commander of 4th Company Bavarian Reserve Infantry Regiment 8, was captured with some of his men in Schwaben Redoubt. He was less lucky, being killed by German artillery fire on the way to the British lines.

Initially the situation north of Thiepval was obscure. So swiftly had the forward defenders of Sectors C2 and C3 been overwhelmed, that it was some time before the situation was fully clarified. A further complication came about because an early report received in the Divisional Headquarters stated,

Our own troops are attacking in the direction of Authuille.

In reality, what had been observed was the sight of German prisoners being conducted to the rear. However, an observation post of Reserve Infantry Regiment 119 on the northern bank of the Ancre eventually spotted that the British had succeeded in overrunning the Schwaben Redoubt. The information was passed directly to the Divisional Commander of the 26th Reserve Division, who lost no time in issuing the order for a counter-attack. Had telephone links been available to the 2nd Recruit Company of Infantry Regiment 180, which was occupying the Second Position, there might have been less delay.

Leutnant Scheurlen 2nd Recruit Company Infantry Regiment 18019.

'About 9.00 am British officers were seen orientating themselves with the aid of maps and detachments of British soldiers were observed. Some were digging in and others were advancing into the area in front of Schnürlen's Company (1st Recruit Company Infantry Regiment 180). Fire brought to bear by Schnürlen's Company and one weapon of the 1st Machine Gun Company Reserve Infantry Regiment 119 caused the enemy to pull back into the Hansastellung [Hanseatic Position] and Schwaben Redoubt.'

The possibility of such a dangerous development had been foreseen. In keeping with normal practice, counter-attack plans would almost certainly have been laid in advance and a Warning Order had been sent down

through the chain of command on 27th June:

'At 12.00 midday today the Brigade [52 Reserve] received Operation Order No. 2453 from [26th Reserve] Division that Sector Thiepval North is to be reinforced as necessary. If the enemy gets established there, he is to be ejected at once. Further elements of 1st Battalion Bavarian Reserve Infantry Regiment 8 can be made available to replace troops moved forward out of the Intermediate or Second Position for this purpose...'

This order had led to the reinforcement of the Second Position by elements of Bavarian Reserve Infantry Regiment 8 and the Recruit Companies of Infantry Regiment 18021 and the placement of 4th Company Bavarian Reserve Infantry Regiment 8 in Schwaben Redoubt, which brought the number of defenders up to between 400 and 500 – not too large a number for a stronghold with a 500 metre frontage.

From the start the entire counter-attack proved to be far from simple to mount. Even the distribution of the order was difficult, because there were no telephone links to the dispersed battalions of Bavarian Reserve Infantry Regiment 8. However Reserve Leutnant Trainé of the Württemberg Reserve Dragoons was available at Divisional Headquarters for such an eventuality and he took the orders in person. The counter-attack was planned to be conducted by three groups, under the overall command of Oberstleutnant Bram, Commander of Bavarian Reserve Infantry Regiment 8. The grouping was intended to be as follows:

Group 1
Major Prager Commanding Officer 1st Battalion Bavarian Reserve Infantry Regiment 8. 2nd Company Bavarian Reserve Infantry Regiment 8, 1st and 2nd Recruit Companies Infantry Regiment 180, Engineer Company Schofeld and 1st Machine Gun Company Reserve Infantry Regiment 119. (Attack from the northern section of the Second Position against Schwaben Redoubt.)

Group 2
Major Beyerköhler Commanding Officer 3rd Battalion Bavarian Reserve Infantry Regiment 8. 3rd, 11th and 12th Companies Bavarian Reserve Infantry Regiment 8. Machine Gun Sharp Shooter Troop 89. (Attack towards Schwaben Redoubt from Hill 153.)

Group 3
Major Roesch Commanding Officer 2nd Battalion Bavarian Reserve Infantry Regiment 8. 2nd Battalion Bavarian Reserve Infantry Regiment 8. (Attack on Schwaben Redoubt via Stuff Redoubt.)

At 9.55 a.m., Major Roesch received the following order directly from Headquarters 26th Reserve Division:

Enemy has forced his way into Schwaben Redoubt. 2nd Battalion Bavarian Reserve Infantry Regiment 8, with 1st Machine Gun Company and one platoon of the 'Musketen'

Company is subordinated to 52 Reserve Infantry Brigade. The Battalion is to move immediately, dealing with any enemy encountered, to the Ancre Valley and is to advance to the Second Position via Stallmulde [Stable Hollow]*. Sector South I to South III is to be occupied and held, with main effort on the right flank. 52 Reserve Infantry Brigade will be kept informed from here. Signed: Freiherr von Soden.

The battalion, which had been standing by in Irles since 5.30 a.m. ready to move, set off, but such was the weight of artillery fire directed against the rear areas that it was not until 3.00 p.m. that it reached Stable Hollow near Grandcourt.

The serious news concerning the loss of Schwaben Redoubt swiftly reached Headquarters XIV Reserve Corps, where Generalleutnant von Stein lost no time in ordering a speeding up of the attack. By 10.45 a.m. an amendment to the 26th Reserve Division Operation Order had been received and was being processed at Headquarters 52 Reserve Infantry Brigade:

Generalleutnant Freiherr von Soden, the brilliant Commander of 26th Reserve Division, who was the primary architect of the bloodiest day in British military history.

'*The Corps Commander has ordered that Schwaben Redoubt is to be recaptured at all costs. To that end the arrival of 2nd Battalion Bavarian Reserve Infantry Regiment 8 is not to be awaited. Rather the attack is to be launched with forces from the Second Position.*'

The Brigade Commander carried out a quick appreciation and issued the following order at 10.50 a.m. to 1st Battalion Bavarian Reserve Infantry Regiment:

'*The British have forced their way into the Hanseatic Position and Schwaben Redoubt. Major Prager, with Companies Schmeißer, Schnürlen, Hudelmeier and Engineer Company Schofeld, together with 1st Machine Gun Company of Reserve Infantry Regiment 119 and Sharp Shooter Troop 89, are to conduct this attack from the right flank of the Second Position. Major Beyerköhler will advance on Schwaben Redoubt from Hill 153 with three companies.*'

Meanwhile time passed as efforts were made to get the necessary orders to all those concerned and the designated units struggled to their start lines through churned up, 'unbelievably muddy' - ground and extraordinarily heavy artillery fire. Oberstleutnant Bram finally arrived at 2.00 p.m. at Stuff Redoubt to take control of the operation. More than two and a half

hours had elapsed since he had received his orders at Headquarters 26th Reserve Division; heavy artillery fire having forced him to move on foot from Pys via Courcelette, where he had received a further briefing from Generalleutnant von Auwärter. It hardly mattered. Group 1 under Major Prager still had not received the order to attack. That did not finally arrive until well after 3.00 p.m., but prior to that Major Prager had already been developing his own plans. Initially he had intended to make use of both the Recruit Companies, but once he finally saw the order, he stood down 1st Recruit Company at 3.13 p.m. Group 2 under Major Beyerköhler, which had received its orders at 11.30 a.m., was furthest advanced, but still not in position and Group 3 under Major Roesch was struggling to make its way forward. In fact this battalion had suffered heavy casualties as a result of artillery fire and was scattered. The 8th Company lost all contact during the advance and ended up in the area of 51 Reserve Infantry Brigade, whence it was despatched with forty engineers to reinforce Saint Pierre Divion. This was just an extreme example. The three assault groups were never united and so the attack never had any chance of developing synergy.

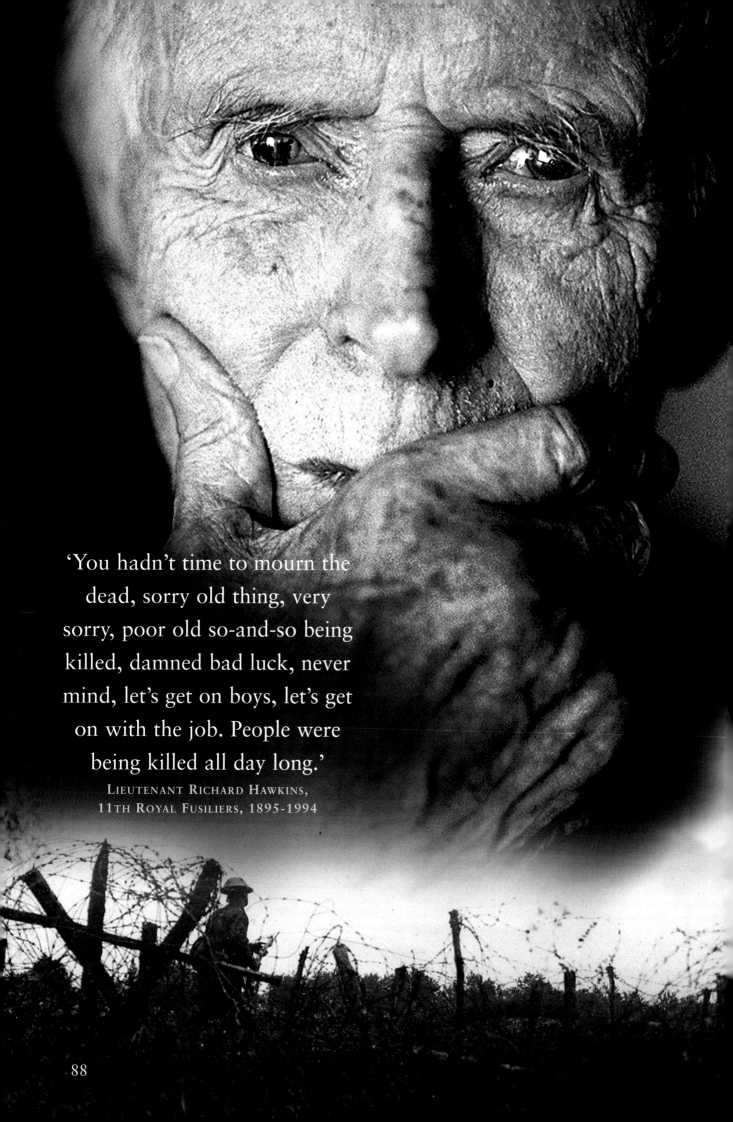

'You hadn't time to mourn the dead, sorry old thing, very sorry, poor old so-and-so being killed, damned bad luck, never mind, let's get on boys, let's get on with the job. People were being killed all day long.'

LIEUTENANT RICHARD HAWKINS,
11TH ROYAL FUSILIERS, 1895-1994

BRITAIN'S LAST TOMMIES ON THE SOMME 1916

'We realized that we were in for a battle, no doubt about that. Everything was building up to such a vast scale that we were all convinced that this was the push, the "Big Push" that was to end the war.' PRIVATE TOM DEWING, 34TH DIVISIONAL ROYAL ENGINEERS SIGNAL COMPANY, 1896-2001

By Richard van Emden

This article was extracted from Richard van Emden's book, *Britain's Last Tommies: Final Memories from Soldiers of the 1914-18 In Their Own Words* and is reproduced here by permission of Pen and Sword Books Ltd.

LIEUTENANT NORMAN DILLON, 14TH NORTHUMBERLAND FUSILIERS, 1896-1997

I had heard that my battalion was going to take part in the attack and I wanted to be in it as we believed this was the big one. I couldn't see any future to tunnelling if open warfare was going to resume and we were on the move, as I hoped we would be. So I put in a request to go back to my unit and they had no grounds to refuse it.

The 14th Northumberland Fusiliers, being pioneers, had to follow the leading troops at some distance, the object being to help consolidate the newly-won positions, but on the day it was all badly managed. We were to enlarge scrapes in the ground or turn captured German trenches round to face the other way, so that the parados became the parapet, and then put out barbed wire.

On the morning of 1st July I was half a mile away when these huge mines were exploded, and the ground shook under my feet. The first waves went over the top and made some progress. I saw a field gun battery galloping up and putting its guns into position and firing just behind what had been our front line. Those guns soon had to limber up and gallop off again because they came under fire; they were too close. I went forward with my company about half a mile, and found one of the junior subalterns, Second Lieutenant Walker, had been needlessly killed after being brought up, then doing nothing, before he was hit by desultory bursts of machine-gun fire on our flanks. The truth is we hadn't much idea what we were to do that day because everybody expected to be miles ahead.

PRIVATE TOM DEWING, 34TH DIVISION, ROYAL ENGINEERS SIGNAL COMPANY, 1896-2001

On 30th June, the day before the attack, two of us were sent to an observation post called Smiths Redoubt. This was a small dugout with a slot that enabled us to look over the German lines. There we were joined by the Brigade Intelligence Officer, Lieutenant 'Blanco' White, and various runners. We were also connected to Brigade Headquarters by telephone, and had a powerful telescope that could be mounted on a tripod.

Shortly before 7.30 a.m. on 1st July we felt the ground heave from the explosion of the mine at La Boisselle but we could see nothing. In the first place, there was a certain amount of mist and then when you add to that the enormous amount of smoke from the barrage, a great deal was hidden. Then when the mist and smoke cleared, we were able to see the infantry going forward in open formation as if on the parade ground. In many cases the men didn't get very far, they were just wiped out. One of the officers in our dugout had some field glasses which he allowed us to use from time to time, and looking into the crater we could sometimes see a German getting up, raising his rifle and firing. During the attack, a signaller, Corporal Bone, and one or two other men followed the infantry to their first objective.

They set up a heliograph, as the weather was ideal for its use, and we waited anxiously for the first flash. When it came, we were thrilled; they had reached their objective. They sent our call sign, 'ZJA, ZJA'. Z stood for Brigade, J was the tenth letter of the alphabet, A the first, so we got 101st Brigade. We waited for the message that was to follow but it never came. The enemy had seen the flashing and opened up with a machine gun.

SERGEANT WALTER JAMES POPPLE, NO14134, 15 PLATOON, D COMPANY, 8TH KING'S OWN YORKSHIRE LIGHT INFANTRY, 16 JANUARY 1896-CIRCA 1990

1st July promised to be a beautiful day. The sun had risen high in the sky and we could hear the birds singing. I stood on the firestep and scanned the scene. Jerry had been pounded for a week and would be decimated. What few were left would not be able to offer any real resistance. I recall wondering if that was true as a shell burst in the trench forty yards away, and an officer and three men were killed outright.

A loud blast on a whistle and the first wave began the attack, as the barrage moved forward. Then it was time for my platoon to go. A line had been cut in the barbed wire the night before, through which to advance, but as I did so I could scarcely believe my eyes.

The first three lines were being mown down. I walked forward in a daze. Near the crest of the slope, I saw the reason for the carnage: Jerry had manned every single post. As I neared the enemy wire, I felt a sharp thud accompanied by a pain in my chest and I fell.

PRIVATE CLARRIE JARMAN, 7TH QUEEN'S (ROYAL WEST SURREY REGIMENT), 1896-1996

That morning we turned out our pockets, dumping postcards of naked French girls to ensure they weren't sent home with any personal effects should we be killed. Then the trench ladders were put into place and on the blast of whistles, and after wishing our chums the best of luck, over we went. It was like a dream, lots of the lads were shot down just going over the parapet.

We advanced, each platoon forming a star. Only when we got close to the German line would we move into extended order. But of course it was just a shambles; it was every man for himself.

I was a bomber. I was staggering along with 250 rounds of small arms ammunition, a rifle and a fixed bayonet, seven mills bombs on my chest and seven on my back and a pick and shovel, going along in a dream-like state. All the while you could hear the machine guns, tak, tak, tak, tak, tak.

Lieutenant Haggard had taken us over, one of two brothers in the battalion. The last I saw of him, he was bending over a local chap, Arthur Spooner, who had lost an eye, and shortly after, about half way across, I got hit.

I went down straightaway and crawled into a deep shell hole, dumping all my equipment. I had a look round the battleground and as far as I could see, there were our lads lying out dead, wounded and dying. There were some lads in a shell hole near me and when they saw me looking over, they said, 'Get your head down' and I did and didn't know any more. The shrapnel had shattered the bottom part of my right leg and for much of the time I was unconscious with the loss of blood. There was no pain and I lay there all that day, about fourteen hours.

It was getting dusk when a lad from the RAMC happened to come my way looking for wounded, and in a very faint voice I called to him and he heard my call. I was lucky to be picked up.

LIEUTENANT RICHARD HAWKINS, 11TH ROYAL FUSILIERS, 1895-1994

We moved up into our front line trench, and in the early hours every man was given a good breakfast and packet of Woodbines, stupid thing to say, but I went over smoking an Abdullah cigarette. It was a lovely morning and over the top we went at zero hour. We had a marvellous day, and got right into their first and second line trenches. The Manchesters to our left were held up and the battalions were held up on our right too, otherwise, someone said, we could have walked through to Berlin.

I was keen to get on and beat the enemy. I didn't really think I might be hit at any moment. My batman, named Good, followed me over and he was hit early on; we were great friends, damn good chap. He slumped to the ground and appeared to have been shot through the lungs. I thought he was dying, but I had to leave him, I'd got to get on with the war.

You hadn't time to mourn the dead, sorry old thing, very sorry, poor old so-and-so being killed, damned bad luck, never mind, let's get on boys, let's get on with the job. People were being killed all day long.

PRIVATE JOE YARWOOD, 94TH FIELD AMBULANCE, ROYAL ARMY MEDICAL CORPS, 1896-1995

We were taking the wounded from a relay post at the end of the communication trench across Euston Dump to the main road, where the dugouts were. Some of the injured had blighty wounds and you could almost see the satisfaction on their faces. The machine-gun bullets were flying all around, all the time. If a chap was able to walk, it was much better for him to walk than to occupy a stretcher, and where we could, we would carry his equipment and escort him down. I met one poor devil injured in the face. He had been a walking wounded case and he was an elderly man, too, and I felt very sorry for him. His face was bandaged but his wound was still bleeding, and the whole of his chest was covered with a thick mat of congealed blood. I thought he would go down any minute with loss of blood. I couldn't help him because I'd already got a case with me, but I got him carried out on a stretcher because, had he collapsed, he might well have died. And that's what I was doing, all day long, simply going backwards and forwards like an automaton, you didn't think much. If we'd been

Stretcher bearers taking a wounded Tommy off the front line, passing the bodies of dead British soldiers that are awaiting removal.

winning, that might have been some consolation, but we hadn't even got that.

There were so many more lying out in No Man's Land, but we couldn't reach them. We talked about it. One team tried to clamber out over the top, but one of the lads was shot straightaway, a bullet smashing his thigh, and the rest of the team scrambled back in. We were amazed that Jerry was able to survive the bombardment.

SERGEANT WALTER POPPLE, 8TH KING'S OWN YORKSHIRE LIGHT INFANTRY, 1896-1990

Running footsteps to my rear seemed to bring me back to reality. Then came the sound of a falling body, and with it the certain knowledge that a sniper was about. A German was firing from an advanced post, picking off anyone he saw, including the wounded. As I glanced upwards, he saw me. He fired, a bullet taking the heel off my boot. My rifle was somewhere around but my shoulder was so stiff that I couldn't handle it. Then there were the two grenades in my tunic pockets but I couldn't throw them that distance. All these thoughts flashed through my mind with the ugly realization that any pot shots might easily set off the grenades.

I came to the terrible decision that it was better to get it over with quickly and die, rather than to be picked off piece by piece so I raised my head and pushed myself upwards, almost kneeling to look straight down into the muzzle of his rifle. A sharp crack, and my helmet flew off and my neck stiffened. I sank to the ground. Utter silence. The hours passed by. At first there was a buzzing sensation in my head and then sharp piercing darts of pain. Had I been killed as I first thought? I dared not lift my head and there I remained through the heat of the day, wondering if in fact part of my head had been blown away. Night came, and I cautiously turned over and began to take stock. I gently lowered the bandolier full of ammunition from my shoulders, and the two hand grenades. Moving on my hands and knees, I crept to a large shell hole and despite the bodies around it, began to make myself comfortable. The bullet, I realized, had hit flush on the front of my helmet but instead of killing me outright it must have ricocheted upwards with such force that it ripped the straps from the flanges on my shrapnel helmet, sending it spinning into the air. The Germans, of course, would have assumed that I was dead.

All through the night, incessant calls were being made for stretcher bearers interspersed by rifle and machine-gun fire.

The next day followed the same pattern except that we were shelling Jerry's front line trenches with high explosive shrapnel that at times crossed the shell hole where I was sheltering, wounding me in the right leg and shoulders, some seven more wounds in all.

LIEUTENANT RICHARD HAWKINS, 11TH ROYAL FUSILIERS, 1895-1994

General Maxse came to see us afterwards. He was about five foot six tall and, rather stupidly, we thought, he had a guardsman as his aide-de-camp, Captain Montague, who was about six foot three.

Maxse spoke to us: 'Morning, gentlemen, damn good show, thank you very much, you did very well, marvellous. Tell me, where would you expect to find a group of officers congregated together in the middle of the biggest battle there has ever been?' 'Ooh,' we thought, 'now, wait a minute.' 'I'll tell you,' he said. 'walking about on the skyline looking for souvenirs! I saw them through my field glasses.' Well, there wasn't anything else to do, all was peace and quietness where we were and I managed to pick up a marvellous German Pickelhaube.

We had a good day on 1st July, no doubt about it. As for my batman Good, he was picked up later in the day and the wound was nothing like as bad as I'd feared. He wrote to me from hospital about my new batman, a Northerner. 'I hear you've got Green doing for you now, Sir, he's a good lad but it's a pity he don't speak our language.' Marvellous fellow. Became a police sergeant on the other side of London somewhere.

[Ed. The 11th Royal Fusiliers were one of the more fortunate battalions in action that day. Casualties were relatively light and German resistance in the trenches attacked by the Fusiliers was less determined than on other parts of the front.]

PRIVATE TOM DEWING, 34TH DIVISION ROYAL ENGINEERS SIGNAL COMPANY, 1896-2001

We didn't realize what had happened until afterwards, until the next church parade. At Brigade Headquarters we had regular church parades, and on this occasion, instead of the troops coming along as they usually did, there was just a handful out of each battalion. We felt sick. The colonels were sitting in front of what was left of their men, sobbing. The service was taken by Padre Black, who later became Dr James Black, Moderator of the Church of Scotland. He was a man we all respected; he was more likely to be found in the trenches than in the officers' mess. Before the attack started, he had said that he would go over the top with the stretcher bearers but the message through our signal office said, 'If Padre Black goes over the top, he is to be arrested and sent down the line for a court martial.' Instead, he did the next best thing. He stayed at the first field dressing station.

How he managed to take that service, I don't know. His text was 'I will restore unto you the years that the locusts have eaten'. He meant every word of his sermon, and we knew it. There were so few, so few men left. How can you describe a mere handful of men where you used to see about a battalion? It must have been a great

'I will restore unto you the years that the locusts have eaten.'

ordeal for him to conduct that service. It is an occasion that I shall always remember.

LIEUTENANT RICHARD HAWKINS, 11TH ROYAL FUSILIERS, 1895-1994

I was lying out on the night of the 1st of July in the dark, half asleep, happy and with nothing to do, and a voice in the dark said, 'Hello, had a good day?' 'Oh,' I said 'yes.' 'Do you know where the 12th Middlesex are?' I said, 'I don't know where the hell they are, somewhere on the right, I think.' 'Oh,' he said, 'I'm Colonel Maxwell and I've come to take over the 12th Middlesex.' He'd come up in the middle of the night to see where the battalion was. Oops, in the dark I didn't realize he was a colonel. He couldn't wait until his battalion came out of the line, he had to come up and join it, not because he had to, but because he could not keep out of the battle.

PRIVATE JOE YARWOOD, 94TH FIELD AMBULANCE, ROYAL ARMY MEDICAL CORPS, 1896-1995

The next day the wounded were still waiting to be moved away, but we were lacking convoys. All these elephant dugouts had been turned into aid posts. There were piles of wounded lying on stretchers waiting for ambulances to move them.

I had just left the dressing station when we were shelled, but they landed with a pop not an explosion, and then I got a whiff of it, it was tear gas. I rushed back to lend a hand in getting as many under cover as I could. They couldn't get their gas masks on, so for an hour or so it was pandemonium trying to get these poor devils out of harm's way.

Our colonel, an Irishman by the name of Stewart, was a bit of a martinet and inclined to shout and bark and call you a bloody fool. He was very ambitious, a doctor in civilian life, and he held the DSO and MC and you don't get those for nothing. A brilliant officer, no doubt, but he was, to my mind, a little conceited, haughty even, you get it with some officers who take a large size in hats. Anyway, when we were leaving the trenches, he sounded like a benevolent father, pleased and very pleasant for once because we'd broken all records with the number of wounded we'd shifted, although he couldn't quite show his gratitude.

We were told to clear out because our lot was decimated. I saw a battalion leaving and there was a band in front and then about three or four ranks of soldiers, and that was all that was left of a thousand: thirty or forty men.

Just around there I recall one poor devil who had been buried in the bottom of the trench, but not deep enough, with the result that the top of his skull was exposed just level with the top of the trench floor. There was a bald patch right down the centre of the poor fellow's skull where troops had marched and worn the hair off his head. My God, what would his relatives at home think if they knew that had happened?

SERGEANT WALTER POPPLE, 8TH KING'S OWN YORKSHIRE LIGHT INFANTRY, 1896-1990

The third day I was exhausted, and it was on this day that a thunderstorm broke the terrific heat. By this time all the bodies around me had turned black. One of them had a waterproof sheet protruding at the back of his pack. I formed a ridge and the water trickled down into my mouth. The fourth day was relatively quiet but I realized time was getting short and unless help arrived soon, I was finished. I made up my mind that, whatever happened, I must reach my lines by morning. Crawling throughout the night, I got to within a few yards of our trenches by daybreak. By a sustained effort, I rose to my feet and hopped the necessary distance. Machine guns opened out, but I held my course and was lucky to enter one of the lanes cut for the attack. A sentry shouted, 'Who's there?' I croaked 'KOYLI.' To hear my own tongue being spoken was nectar. 'And yours?' 'Middlesex' came the reply, 'anyone else out there?' I told him no.

[Ed. Walter arrived back in the front line on the morning of 5th July, and must have been one of the very last men wounded on 1st July to have remained on the battlefield unattended. The bullet that hit him in the shoulder was removed and he kept it as a souvenir. However, the psychological effect on Walter's health was devastating. He lost weight and looked gaunt, and although he recovered from his wounds medically, he was in no fit state to return to active service. In 1917 he was removed from a parade of men due to return to France, as he was clearly in distress. He never returned to the firing line. The memory of those days haunted Walter, before in 1986, aged ninety, he finally returned to France and the Somme battlefield.]

CORPORAL NORMAN EDWARDS, 1/6TH GLOUCESTERSHIRE REGIMENT, 1894-1999

We took over the sector behind the village of Serre on 5th July from the 94th Brigade and at night time, when I looked out, the flares were all going up, and between the lines, in No Man's Land, there were twinkling lights everywhere. I thought, twinkling lights, what could it be? I found out afterwards the Pals Battalions of 31st Division had arranged that every man would carry a triangular piece of tin on the back of his pack so that when he was crawling forward, attacking, our own airmen looking down could see the depth of the advance. All those twinkling lights were literally hundreds of men who had been killed on that morning, before breakfast, awful slaughter. You can understand what a man felt like to see that. I just thanked God we hadn't been ordered to attack, although

had we been ordered to do so we would have done our duty, I would think, because we'd got to win the war.

[Ed. After a brief respite, fighting resumed on the southern sector of the Somme battlefield, where the attacks on 1st July had seen a modicum of success, two villages, Montauban and Mametz, having fallen that first day. On 2nd July, the Germans abandoned another village, Fricourt, and a day later fresh attacks resulted in the talking of La Boisselle. Assaults of a limited nature continued, before a major night attack was conducted on the 14th on the German second line with positive results; a further phase of the Somme campaign was opened up on the 23rd July.]

TROOPER SMILER MARSHALL, 1/1ST ESSEX YEOMANRY, 1897-2005

The Ox and Bucks arrived between five and six in the afternoon and were billeted close to where we were, in broken-down houses in Mametz Village. They were to attack the next day. Zero hour was 6.30 a.m. and their objective was not far from Mametz Wood.

It was the worst place I ever saw; there was more dead laid there than I ever saw anywhere, and we buried them. The Ox and Bucks went over the next morning at 6.30 a.m. and by 8 a.m. there was hardly one left. The next night we were sent up as a working party to help bury them, one, two and three in a shell hole. I didn't go through their pockets, that wasn't my job, but one of these dead chaps, he had pictures of his girlfriend and his mother, letters with his address, and these were all sticking out of his pocket or lying on the ground by his body, because shrapnel or machine-gun bullets had ripped it open. I took his new boots off and put him in a shell hole, and threw my old boots in the shell hole with him, and took his. A while later I wrote to his mother in High Wycombe, Turner, I think the name was, and I got a nice letter from her. She said he had been reported missing in action. I said that I was on a burying party and told her he was killed near Mametz Wood and that we buried him in No Man's Land. Blimey, it was a rough job, poor buggers, but you just had to get on with it and not think.

We were taken on working parties for several nights and I got hit through the hand, because the bullets and shrapnel were flying around, battle or no battle. You don't know what caused it until you see the blood running onto the ground. I was sent down to the casualty clearing station, walked down. There must have been some dirt as well because my whole hand turned to poison, and it got worse and worse and ached all up my arm. Eventually I got sent to Rouen and then back to England and Newcastle. I nearly lost my arm.

[Ed. Between 25th and 31st July, a large number of men from the 3rd Cavalry Division were sent to help dig trenches between Mametz Wood and the village of Contalmaison. These included around eighty men from the Essex Yeomanry. Nearby, the 1/4th Oxfordshire and Buckinghamshire Light Infantry had made an attack on 23rd July, losing a large number of men, including two bearing the name of Turner.]

RIFLEMAN ROBERT RENWICK, MM, 16TH KING'S ROYAL RIFLE CORPS, 1896-1997

All the woods round the Somme were hard fought for, Mametz Wood, High Wood. It was after my battalion had attacked High Wood and lost a lot of men, that I was sent to France on a draft just in time for an attack on Delville Wood, or Devil's Wood as it was called, and for good reason.

We were due to go over at a specific time but our bombardment fell short onto our lines so the officer said, 'I'll be damned if I'll see my own men knocked out by our artillery,' and he took us out and led us into shell holes. We waited for the barrage to lift and we advanced. The wood was just a mess, there was no undergrowth at all. A number of men were falling and I looked around to see a man hiding his corporal's stripes. I think he thought he wouldn't be targetted by the Germans without them. Then, as we dodged about from shell hole to shell hole I had a strange vision. I saw myself back at school and our schoolmaster was coming down his garden path to the wicket to call us in and line us up. I said to myself, 'I think if ever you see that place again, you'll be lucky.'

After the battle, we were sent back to bury the dead. Being sent back to bury your own pals, I think they did that

to harden us up a little bit, but I thought it was rough. It was mainly men from the new draft who were sent to do it, but I thought men from a labour platoon should have done it. We took the dog tags off, and buried the men in their groundsheets.

One of the dead was a lad who had a web belt and a purse with a golden sovereign in it. He'd showed it to us a few times but I couldn't bring myself to take it out. That lad was buried with the sovereign. Later in the war, I would have taken it out, but not then.

A curious incident happened after this. There was a lad who got home wounded and he wrote to my parents explaining how I'd been killed. During the attack he had shouted to me that so-and-so had been injured and was in his shell hole, and he told my parents that I'd come across to see if there was anything I could do. Then he shouted back to my mates, 'Renwick's been killed now', and he wrote all this in a note to my mother and father. I don't know how that happened. Perhaps there was another lad of the same name.

I remember the incident but I certainly wasn't killed. My father read the note first and then handed it to my mother, and she got a terrific shock. Then he said, 'Look, we've had a field card since this date, so this cannot be right.' It was a mystery, that one.

[Ed. The only other Rifleman Renwick killed while serving with the 16th Kings Royal Rifle Corps died of wounds on 15th July, following the attack on High Wood, which is close to Delville Wood. His name was Joseph Renwick, and he came from Gateshead.]

PRIVATE DICK TRAFFORD, 1/9TH KING'S LIVERPOOL REGIMENT, 1898-1999

The rations were being dished out when the sergeant came up with a loaf of bread and some jam. The loaf was divided up and we held our mess tin lids out for our jam ration just as a shrapnel shell burst overhead. One bit of shrapnel went through the jam and my mess tin lid, another chunk cut part of my thumb off, and I had three other wounds on the same hand. The man next to me got a piece through his back, which killed him outright. Another chap was shocked but all right, but the fourth lad, Joe Shaw, he jumped up on top of the road and ran off towards the end of our line, shouting and bawling, waving his arms. We couldn't really make out what he was saying because he was shell-shocked, but this was right in front of the German lines and that was the last we heard of him. We thought naturally that the Germans would get him; he made a good target for any machine gunner.

About three months later, I was on leave in Ormskirk and I was walking down the road, just as a chap in a postman's uniform crossed in front of me, all smiles. 'Hello, Dick, don't you know me?' I says, 'I know the voice,' and it was this Joe Shaw. I said, 'I thought you were dead.'

During the fighting, the army had a little place in a wood about three miles back from the trenches, where they could put these sorts of cases temporarily, to see if they could recover. However, Joe was sent down to the dressing station, but there were that many wounded, he was bundled in with the others onto a train and sent down the line to hospital. He was shell-shocked, there was no doubt about it, and in the end he was considered of no further use for the army and was demobilized.

PRIVATE TED FRANCIS, 16TH WARWICKSHIRE REGIMENT, 1896-1996

On the Somme I saw lots of people in attacks, where you had to go from one shell hole to another towards the enemy, and you'd find people stopping where they were and not attempting to move and giving the officers and NCOs the idea that they were shell-shocked – that was common – and an officer or an NCO would almost kick them out of the hole and tell them to go forward with the other chaps. Everyone was afraid, but as a matter of fact my brother Harry and I, seeing other people who couldn't stand it made us a little bit braver, we felt good that they couldn't stand this sort of thing but we could.

LIEUTENANT RICHARD HAWKINS, 11TH ROYAL FUSILIERS, 1895-1994

After the battle of Thiepval, we were withdrawn to a cellar in a château. I spent the night there with Colonel Maxwell, commanding the 12th Middlesex. He was, as ever, passionately fond of war and fighting, and couldn't really understand those who weren't.

While we were there, one of the boys had a bit of shell-shock and kept running across the road, and Colonel Maxwell said to me, 'Give him a damn good kick up the backside as he passes you, he'll be all right,' so I did, and he was, he was all right.

Maxwell had got a Victoria Cross in some obscure war and had been ADC to Kitchener in India. That evening, he told me he'd been serving in India when war broke out and immediately had asked to be sent to France. When he was told to wait until orders, he said, 'If you don't make arrangements for me to go, I shall desert.' So they allowed him to go and in the end he was given command of the Middlesex.

In that attack on Thiepval, I'd had a shell land literally at my feet, but it didn't go off and that caused me to be a bit muzzy myself for a time. But Maxwell, he didn't understand the word fear at all. I heard him once say to my commanding officer. 'You know, Carr, I don't think you really enjoy this war, do you?' Carr said, 'My God, I do not, I think it is a dreadful business.' 'No?' Maxwell said, 'I thoroughly enjoy it.'

He was killed in 1917 when, holding the rank of brigadier general, he was hit walking over the top where he shouldn't have been; he just could not keep out of it.

[Ed. Francis Aylmer Maxwell won his Victoria Cross during the conflict in South Africa. In March 1900, the then Lieutenant Maxwell attempted to retrieve a battery of guns and a number of limbers under enemy fire. On five occasions he went back, helping to save two guns and three limbers.]

PRIVATE EDWARD ALBION LEONARD WHITE, NO12265, C COMPANY, 10TH KING'S ROYAL RIFLE CORPS, 16 OCTOBER 1897-FEBRUARY 1999

I really broke lose when my mate Bobby was killed, that hurt me more than anything. He was one of a draft sent out to the company, just as I'd been in 1915, and he tacked on to me. 'On your own? Want company?' and that was it, mates. The bullet that got him must have shot across my breast and stopped with him. That was at Ypres. They carried him off on a stretcher. After I lost my pal, I did swear that I would kill, kill, kill and believe me, I did what I intended to do.

Guillemont, 3 September 1916: two minutes to zero, the whistle blew and I was going to do what I intended to do. I ran and we stormed their lines, we went right through before the Germans even knew we were coming. I killed two. 'Sprechen sie Deutsch?' One chap shouted out 'Ja'. He stood up and I set my rifle and I fired twice and he screamed and went down. I saw another. 'Sprechen sie Deutsch? Sprechen sie Deutsch?' A long time before I got an answer, 'Ja wohl', and he got up, blimey he was as big as a house. I pulled the trigger. I had a look round, nothing moving, they must have been on their own. 'Sprechen sie Deutsch?' I was still carrying on. I got right in amongst them, I had my rifle and I was firing. Put another clip in, my God, you never heard such screaming in all your life.

I did not see someone was behind me, I didn't know, I was young you know, very, very young. Somebody came up on my left shoulder, I looked, I couldn't do anything, he was too far on top of me, and he just opened up. He blew me, he really, truly, he blew me in the air. I can remember my rifle going one way and I was going the

A young British infantryman killed during the attack at Guillemont. Scenes like this were to haunt the veterans for the rest of their lives.

other, straight down, face first into a shell hole. I lay there and turned on my back. Three wounded Germans were down there, and one put his hand out to me.

Nobody came to help me for a long time and then all of a sudden somebody slid down this shell hole. 'Need any help, chum?' I can remember his words. I said, 'My arm.' He had a red cross on his sleeve. 'He's only a boy,' that's what I heard. I got on my feet, I scratched my way up to the top.

As I walked back, someone spoke to me. Really and truly, I was in such a daze, I wasn't interested in anything. He was a sergeant, and he had a bullet through his neck, lucky bugger, it must have missed his windpipe, so I tagged along with him. A truck came along and he pulled up. 'Come on, lads, you can't walk all that way. I'll give you a lift in the back.' He helped me up and we started to roll. I was moaning with the pain, and I was told to shut up.

The lorry rolled and rolled and stopped. The driver came round the back. 'Come on, lads, this is as far as we go.' I've never been so surprised in all my life. Huts, lines of huts from here to kingdom come. A girl came up to me, and said, 'Would you like some bread and dripping, Tommy, and a nice cup of tea?'

[Ed. Clearly still very disturbed by his experiences, Edward talked about this incident as though he was back there. It was a very uncanny experience to listen to him talk in such a way, and he was the only veteran I ever met to do so.]

PRIVATE DICK TRAFFORD, 1/9TH KING'S LIVERPOOL REGIMENT, 1898-1999

We were due to attack Guillemont, and I had orders that I must place my machine gun on top of the trench to cover the attack. I objected as much as I dared to the

An overwhelming sight for medics. Masses of infantrymen await treatment.

officer, that I preferred to go over the top and lie in a shell hole because I had a better chance of covering the men. I could sweep the German parapet with the machine gun and keep their heads down while our bombers lobbed grenades in to the trench. But he wouldn't have it, no, that won't do, instead I must fire over the men's heads all the time. Well, obviously he was in charge. The attack started and I opened fire, carrying out his instructions, and a German sniper must have seen the flashes from the gun because he fired and hit the gun and the bullet ricocheted off and caught me in the throat flat ways, knocking me out. It stopped my breath, I didn't know where I was for some time afterwards. The bullet had slammed into my windpipe and for years and years I had trouble swallowing in fact, even today, [1998] I find I sometimes choke.

I found out afterwards that our men took the trench, but the bombers, the men I'd wanted to cover, were wiped out.

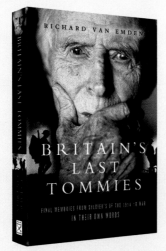

SOMME 1916 THE JOURNEY TO WAR IN COLOUR

PHOTOGRAPHS COLOURED BY JON WILKINSON